FORTUNE'S FAVORITE:
SIR CHARLES DOUGLAS AND
THE BREAKING OF THE LINE

FORTUNE'S FAVORITE:
SIR CHARLES DOUGLAS AND THE BREAKING OF THE LINE

BY

CHRISTOPHER J. VALIN

Fireship Press
www.FireshipPress.com

FORTUNE'S FAVORITE: Sir Charles Douglas and the Breaking of the Line - Copyright © 2009 by Christopher J. Valin

ISBN-13: 978-1-934757-72-7
ISBN-10: 1-934757-72-1

BISAC Subject Headings:

BIO008000	BIOGRAPHY & AUTOBIOGRAPHY / Military
HIS027150	HISTORY / Military / Naval
HIS015000	HISTORY / Europe / Great Britain

6954

Address all correspondence to:
Fireship Press, LLC
P.O. Box 68412
Tucson, AZ 85737

Or visit our website at:
www.FireshipPress.com

1.0

Contents

PREFACE

I've always been very conscious of history. I was born in the Boston area, and I've known about Paul Revere, Minutemen, the Battle of Bunker Hill, and Plymouth Rock for as far back as I can remember. We moved to Colorado while I was in grade school, and when we made our regular treks back to Massachusetts, my parents would take different routes so that my brothers and I could see more places and check out everything from battlefields such as Gettysburg to national treasures like the Liberty Bell. We were very lucky kids. It's no wonder I grew up to be a history teacher.

On the way home during one trip, we went through Quebec (talk about taking the long way), from which my father's family had emigrated at the turn of the last century. It was on this trip to Canada that I first remember hearing from my father that we were related to someone named Sir Howard Douglas, who had been the governor of New Brunswick and was in the Encyclopedia Britannica. My father had heard about him as a child, and even read a book about him that he'd found in the library. The thought of actually having such a tangible connection to history was thrilling to me, and I looked him up the first chance I had. There was some interesting information on him, including the fact that he had been shipwrecked off Newfoundland as a young man, fought Napoleon in the Peninsular War, and was responsible for a number of innovations in naval warfare. But with little else to go on, I filed the information away in the back of my mind for a later time.

That time came in the late-1990s, when I began to be more interested in genealogy, and the broadening of the Internet had made it a much faster and easier hobby. While I was staying with my parents on vacation after having moved to California, my father showed me some old letters, pictures, and genealogical information he had come into his possession of when his father passed away. I discovered that I was not just related to Sir Howard Douglas, I was his great-great-great-great grandson. Actually seeing the list of names going back from my grandfather to Sir Howard, along with photographs of every generation in between and a lithograph of Sir Howard himself, was pure gold for a historian like me. If my great-grandfather had lived into his eighties, I would have known him, and Sir Howard was *his* great-grandfather.

I attempted to do more research online, but found only a few small articles with mostly the same information I already knew. But I also found a genealogy site where one of my distant relatives had expanded on the family tree, including Sir Howard's father. I had seen his name in the Encyclopedia article, but it had never occurred to me to look up Sir Charles Douglas.

Once I did, it began years of both historical and genealogical research. Discovering that my 5x great-grandfather was even more famous than his own son, and had played such an important role in so many historical events, was a life-changing revelation for me. The realization that Sir Charles had never received his due as such a significant figure on the world stage made me want to correct the oversight. Almost more importantly, once I came across the mostly-overlooked evidence about his role in the breaking of the line maneuver at the Battle of the Saints, for which others have received the credit, I felt the need to present said evidence as Sir Howard had done nearly two centuries ago. My goal was to know more about Sir Charles than anyone else in the world—to become the person to whom others referred when they wanted information. I began correcting errors about him and his life that I found on websites and in books, and even created the Wikipedia article on him (which I've since seen copied in numerous other places). Somehow, none of that seemed enough to satisfy the historian and writer in me.

When I went back to school to get my master's degree in military history with a concentration in American Revolution studies, part of my objective was to gain a comprehensive working knowledge of not only the man, but also the events that surrounded him. This culminated in a thesis on Sir Charles Douglas and his role in the American Revolution, which served as the basis for this book. It was, at the same time, one of the most difficult and one of the most enjoyable experiences of my life.

A few people have tried to discourage me from revisiting the breaking of the line controversy, and while I understand and respect their point of view, I don't agree that it is a dead end. It's been said many times that a debate this old can never be completely resolved, and that may be true. But with the number of books, articles, websites, and even television shows out there that discuss the issue, both from the past and in the present, I believe it's become more necessary than ever to attempt to delve into the evidence and learn what we can. Most of the information brought forth by Sir Howard Douglas in his book, *Naval Evolutions: a Memoir*, was not generally available for many years until the University of Michigan scanned their copy (at my personal expense, I might add) and made on-demand copies available for purchase. Many of the journals in which the matter was first debated were nearly impossible to find until they were similarly scanned by Google for their Google Books project. With these resources now readily available, the time has come to reevaluate the evidence rather than simply get our information from secondhand accounts, as has so often been the case in the past.

I would like to thank, first, my parents, Vincent and Kathleen Valin, for cultivating my love of history and learning, and for always being so supportive in everything I do. My friend Brian DeLay at UC Berkeley provided me with invaluable advice and helped a great deal with an earlier paper that eventually became the core of my thesis. My professors at American Military University, most notably Dr. Don Sine, Dr. Geoffrey Shaw, and especially my advisor, Dr. Brett Woods, provided me with the background I needed to accomplish a work such as this. I also had the assistance of some experts in the field, who did everything from answering a few questions and giving their opinions to reading portions of my thesis and providing me with notes: Dr. W.A.B. Douglas, Pieter Van Der Merwe at the National Maritime Museum in London, author James Nelson, and especially Dr. Nicholas Tracy at the University of New Brunswick. For the genealogical research, I am grateful for William Douglas' excellent information at The Douglas Archives website, and to my distant cousin, Rory Cunningham, who not only provided me with some breakthroughs and confirmation in my family research, but corrected a major mistake I had made in my (and Sir Charles') Douglas lineage.

I believe you're supposed to save the best for last in these things. So, finally, and most importantly, I want to thank my wife, Cecille, and my two children, Saylor and Sawyer, who have had to put up with me being busy so often and for so long, while I worked on both my degree and this book, as well as my constant other projects I become involved in. I could not have done it without them.

CHAPTER ONE

INTRODUCTION

Charles Douglas was the kind of naval officer whom contemporaries referred to as one of 'Fortune's favorites'.

William Fowler

Historians and other readers have experienced the American Revolution through the eyes of many of the participants. Usually these figures are some of the best-known military leaders and politicians in history from both sides of the War: Washington and Franklin, Burgoyne and Cornwallis, even Benedict Arnold. Thousands of pages are also written in books and articles about lesser-known figures such as Daniel Morgan and Sir Guy Carleton. Yet still, occasionally, there remains a person who has been all but overlooked in historical circles and is virtually unknown to the general public, but whose actions helped shape the course of history by playing a vital role in one of the world's most important wars. Sir Charles Douglas is just such a person.

Sir Charles Douglas, 1st Baronet of Carr, was born in 1727 to one of the proudest and most influential families in Scotland. He was a direct descendant of the Earls of Morton, and his son's biographer claims he would have inherited that title had a distant relative not produced a son late in life. Regardless, he must have had some education, as evidenced by his ability to speak six languages fluently and his fondness for mathematical computation.[1] His naval career began at the age of twelve and included service in Holland, and for a short time following the Seven Years' War he was in St. Petersburg helping Catherine the Great reorganize the Russian navy. But most of his long and distinguished career was spent in the Royal Navy of Great Britain, and he was involved in many of the most important military moments of the eighteenth century.

Douglas took part in the siege of Louisburg in 1745 as a midshipman. As captain of the *Syren* off Newfoundland, it was he who first reported the French attack on St. John's in 1762 during the Seven Years' War. During the American Revolutionary War, his ship broke through the ice in the Gulf of St. Lawrence and continued up the frozen river to relieve Quebec from the siege of the Americans under Benedict Arnold. He was also the man who was tasked by the British government with cobbling together a fleet of vessels to take back Lake Champlain from the American rebels—what historian William Fowler calls "the Herculean efforts...at St. John's."[2] In *Those Damned Rebels*, Michael Pearson describes the result of those efforts:

> It was a quaint little fleet...a masterpiece of improvisation and engineering. Most of the craft had been dragged up past the rapids in pieces and reassembled on the stocks at St. Johns. Others had been fabricated from original designs that were packed with experimental ideas, such as the movable keel that could be raised through the bottom boards of a flatboat in shallow water.[3]

For his service in Quebec, Douglas was made a baronet, a hereditary title below baron but above a knight, in 1777. He also participated in the Battle of Ushant, and was Admiral Lord Rodney's captain-of-the-fleet (with duties similar to an adjutant general) at the Battle of the Saints on 12 April 1782. He was twice made commander-in-chief of North America at Halifax Station, and became a rear-admiral before his untimely death of apoplexy in 1789.

---

[1] S.W. Fullom, *Life of General Sir Howard Douglas, Bart.: From his Notes, Conversations, and Correspondence* (London: John Murray, 1863), pp. 1-3; Walter Riddell Carre, *Border Memories; or, Sketches of Prominent Men and Women of the Border* (Edinburgh: James Thin, South Bridge, 1876), p. 42.

[2] Fowler, p. 174.

[3] Michael Pearson, *Those Damned Rebels: The American Revolution as Seen Through British Eyes* (Da Capo Press, 1972), p. 185.

Sir Charles' promotion to Flag Rank on September 24, 1787, must have been a subject of some controversy, as the *London Times* mentioned in its announcement on September 26:

> Sir Charles Douglas has been made a Rear-Admiral, for the purpose of having command of a squadron of ships in the fleet now getting ready for sea. This gentleman's name finds in the Admiralty list the 52d in the rank of Captain, so that a great number of old Captains must have been set aside and provided for in some other manner, in order to make way for his promotion. [1]

The following day, another article listed all of the captains promoted to flag, followed by a list of "Captains not promoted in the present Promotions of Field Officers, who were entitled by their seniority." [2] According to the naval biographer John Charnock, it was reported by some that Sir Charles was promoted above other, more senior captains, "at the particular instance, and by the command of his majesty." [3] Douglas must have had quite a reputation for the King to step in and order his promotion under those circumstances.

This reputation, however, was well deserved. One of the first references to Douglas in any context is in a letter from Captain (later Rear Admiral) Richard Tyrell to then-Lord of the Admiralty George Grenville, in which he stated that, "Mr. Douglas my fifth lieutenant...is a good clever sensible man." [4] Dr. James Currie said of him "he is of that temperament of mind to which great men belong." [5] Sir Gilbert Blane, Rodney's physician to the fleet, called him "the most enlightened and scientific naval officer with whom I

---

[1] *London Times*, 26 September 1787

[2] *London Times*, 27 September 1787

[3] John Charnock, *Biographia Navalis; or Impartial Memoirs of the Lives and Characters of Officers of the Navy of Great Britain from the Year 1660 to the Present Time*, vol. VI (London: R. Faulder, 1798), p. 430.

[4] N.A.M. Rodger, *The Wooden World* (New York: W.W. Norton & Company, 1986), p. 336.

[5] James Currie, M.D., *Memoir of the Life, Writings, and Correspondence of James Currie, M.D. F.R.S. of Liverpool*, vol. II, William Wallace Currie, ed. (London: Longman, Rees, Orme, Brown, and Green 1831), p. 111.

was ever acquainted."[1] Naval expert and historian A. T. Mahan referred to him as "an eminent officer of active and ingenious turn of mind."[2] The author George Cupples was particularly complimentary:

> His well-known repute in the sea service of the day resembled that of Sir Sidney Smith or Lord Cochrane afterwards; he was the most indefatigable, not only of his friends, but of naval officers. His singular activity ranged from the minutest mechanical requirements of ships and fleets— their sheathing with copper, their use of carronades, patent gunlocks, safety-rudders and boat-davits, improved signals, and combined tactical evolutions—to the professional bearings of a parliamentary election, or a Cabinet Minister's family connections.[3]

Even Lord Loughborough, the Lord Chancellor when the case on his personal succession was appealed to the House of Lords, had this to say in his legal opinion:

> I will...take it upon me to say, that his mind and inclinations were so attached to his profession, and his zeal and ingenuity for the improvement of the navy so great, that I am convinced he could not have been at rest for any great length of time in any situation, but where he had an opportunity of shewing and putting these in practice.[4]

Although there was a huge controversy in the early part of the 19th Century concerning whether Douglas, Admiral Lord Rodney, or John Clerk of Eldin should receive credit for the idea of breaking the French line at the Battle of the Saints in 1782, what was not in question was the superior firing ability of some of the ships in Rodney's fleet during that battle, and the credit for that deservedly goes to Douglas. Dr. Blane said, "It ought not to be concealed,

---

[1] Sir Gilbert Blane to Philip Stevens. Major-General Godfrey Basil Mundy, *The Life and Correspondence of the Late Admiral Lord Rodney*, *Vol. II.* (London: John Murray, 1830, Elibron Classics reprint, 2007), p. 231.

[2] A. T. Mahan, *The Influence of Sea Power Upon History, 1660-1783* (New York: Barnes & Noble Books, 2004, first published 1890) p. 493.

[3] George Cupples, "Convoying *H.M.S.Brutus*," *Good Things: A Picturesque Magazine for Boys and Girls*, Midsummer 1876v (London: Strahan & Co., 1876), p. 138.

[4] Paton, Thomas S. *Reports of Cases Decided in the House of Lords upon Appeal from Scotland from 1753 to 1813, Volume III* (Edinburgh: T&T Clark, 1853), Appendix, p. 459.

however, (except from our enemies) that we had at this time an advantage over them which we never enjoyed before—I mean the mechanical improvement in working artillery, invented and introduced by Sir Charles Douglas, who on this day acted as first captain to the Commander-in-chief."[1]

Feats of engineering were something for which Douglas would also become famous. He was so confident in his ideas on naval gunnery that he used his own money to change the means of firing the cannons on his ship, the *Duke*, from matches over to flintlocks, as well as widen the field of fire of its guns and make them more stable. As a result, these ships were able to fire their guns more often and more accurately, with less risk of injury to those firing them. *The Barham Papers* contain so many letters from Douglas to Charles Middleton, Lord Barham, at the Admiralty, filled with technical information on these types of improvements, that the editor began to excise portions and simply state that Douglas described things in "tedious detail."[2] But Douglas' suggestions worked. The same alterations made to the *Duke* were made to at least two other ships of Rodney's fleet, the *Formidable* and the *Arrogant*, and after the success at the Battle of the Saints, the entire British fleet eventually followed suit.

Years after his death, the controversy arose regarding who should be credited with the idea to break the French line at the Battle of the Saints, when a Scottish merchant, John Clerk of Eldin, claimed Rodney had been influenced by his book, which had mentioned a similar tactic. Rodney's friends and family quickly refuted the claim, but Sir Charles' son, Sir Howard Douglas, as well as eyewitnesses to the battle, stated that it was Sir Charles who suggested the maneuver to Rodney. The controversy raged through several books and journals at the time, and Sir Howard eventually wrote an entire book concerning the matter.

Douglas' personal life was as turbulent as his military career. He was married three times, and had at total of eight children from his first two wives. His first wife was a Dutch woman named Uranie Lidie Marteilhe, although some sources, including the *Dictionary of Canadian Biography*, call her Lydia Schimmelpinck for

---

[1] Blane to Stevens. Mundy, *Rodney*, p. 239.

[2] Sir John Knox Laughton (ed.), *Letters and Papers of Charles, Lord Barham, Admiral of the Red Squadron, 1758-1813* (London: Navy Records Society, 1907).

some reason. Although it is possible that she was married previously and that was her husband's name, it is highly doubtful, since she was only eighteen at the time of her marriage to Charles. She bore him a son, William Henry Douglas, and a daughter, Lydia Mariana Douglas, and some sources mistakenly attribute his second son, Charles, to his first wife as well. Uranie died in 1769, at the age of thirty-seven, possibly during childbirth since it was the same year her daughter was born.

Douglas' second wife was an Englishwoman named Sarah Wood, daughter of John Wood of Yorkshire, but according to the case in the House of Lords, they married in the West Indies while he was stationed there in 1770. She was the mother of General Sir Howard Douglas, his brothers, Charles and Frederick, and his sisters, Christiana, Sarah, and Anne Irwin. Judging from the dates and from a letter to Lord Barham at the Admiralty, Sarah died soon after Frederick's birth in August of 1779, and Frederick himself on 5 September, in Gosport. In the letter, Douglas states that, "Yesterday on my arrival here, I found my dearly beloved spouse in the silent tomb; my son Frederic (this moment dead) who came into the world of healthy aspect and superior size, dwindled to a mere shadow." [1]

What is known of his third wife, with whom he had no children, is that she was named Jane Baillie and was the daughter of a John and Mary Baillie. There is a great deal of confusion regarding her identity, and her last name has been variously reported as Baillie, Grew, and Brisbaine (although his will confirms the name Baillie, and a document transcribed in Sir Howard's *Naval Evolutions* confirms the first name Jane). It is possible that Jane had been married before to a man named Grew, so that both that name and Baillie are correct. Some sources have mistaken his sister, Helena Baillie, for his third wife because she raised his younger children while he was at sea, and shared the same last name. This is probably not a coincidence, but if and how Helena's husband and Jane were related is a mystery. The name Helen Brisbaine is based on an error in *The Scottish Nation* (1862) where it says she was married to Admiral Sir Charles Douglas when, in fact, she was the wife of Admiral Sir James Douglas. [2] From the letters of his eldest daughter, Lydia, it is clear that she (and perhaps the other chil-

---

[1] *Barham Papers*, p. 270.

[2] William Anderson, *The Scottish Nation: or, the Surnames, Families, Liturature, Honours, and Biographical History of the People of Scotland*, vol. 1 (A. Fullarton & Co., 1862), p. 380.

dren) did not get along with their step-mother. This is further evidenced by the fact that the children continued to be raised by Douglas' sister in Olive Bank (near Edinburgh), Scotland, even after he remarried and maintained a house in Gosport, England.[1]

Lydia married Reverend Richard Bingham against his wishes, and he disinherited her as a result. Bingham was known as something of a con artist and Sir Charles was well aware of his reputation. Following his death, Lydia and Bingham sued for a share of the estate, and the case was appealed until 1796, when it was finally decided against them in the House of Lords. The case is famous because of a letter Lydia wrote shortly before Douglas' death to the renowned economist Adam Smith, a friend and distant relative of Sir Charles, requesting his assistance in reconciling her with her father.[2]

Although he was very close to his sister, Helena Douglas Baillie, and she was obviously a great help in raising his children, she also caused her share of troubles for the family. She was such a gossip that a neighbor in Musselburgh, Elizabeth Chalmers Scott, sued her for defamation, and, after a ten year court battle, won.

Over the years, Sir Charles has appeared in works of fiction, from the story "Convoying H.M.S. *Brutus*," by George Cupples in 1876 to the current Sir Sydney Smith series by Tom Grundner, where he explains his naval gunnery innovations to the crew of a ship on which he is being transported in *The Midshipman Prince*. He even appears, albeit only in recollections of the characters, in Patrick O'Brian's Aubrey-Maturin series of novels. In *The Reverse of the Medal* and *The Nutmeg Consolation*, O'Brian relates how Captain Douglas, his commander when he was a midshipman aboard the *Resolution*, had him disrated and turned before the mast to serve six months as a foremast hand. Aubrey himself explains to Maturin that it was punishment for bringing a girl onboard, but Captain Goole (who also served on the ship as a midshipman at the same time) tells his wife that it was because he stole the captain's tripe. In *Patrick O'Brian's Navy*, Richard O'Neill explains that Captain Douglas is, indeed, supposed to be Sir Charles Douglas. O'Neill also states that the girl in question

---

[1] Letter from Helena Baillie to Sir Charles Douglas, 19 February 1789.

[2] Letter from Lydia Mariana Douglas Bingham to Adam Smith, 20 February 1789.

was Sally M'Puta, by whom Aubrey had an illegitimate son, Sam Panda.

Sir Charles Douglas has two towns named after him, Douglas and Douglastown (on Gaspee), both in Nova Scotia. There are some who claim that Douglastown was actually named after an early surveyor of the area, but it has been researched by local historians and there is no record of a surveyor by that name. A song called "Caillich Ohdar" or "Sir Charles Douglas's Strathspey" was composed in his honor by a musician named Nathaniel Gow and is still a popular song for the bagpipes.[1] A portrait by Henry Singleton hangs in London's National Maritime Museum, and a mezzotint created in 1791 by John Jones based on that portrait is often seen in books in which Douglas is mentioned.

With the glaring exception of Admiral Lord Hood, as well as a couple of officers in Halifax, Sir Charles was well liked and admired by virtually everyone, from friends, relatives, and superiors to foes such as the comte de Grasse. According to *The Gentleman's and London Magazine*, the crew of the *Duke* considered him more of a parent than a captain, and he often gave his own money to crewmembers in need, and made sure that the sick crewmembers were taken care of as well as, if not better than, they would have been on land. The story also claimed he rarely took a carriage anywhere, and some mistook this as being cheap because he was always walking. The reality was that he would calculate the amount he saved every time he would skip the carriage ride and then donate that amount to the poor and unfortunate. In a diary, a Hessian officer, Julius Friedrich von Hille, called Douglas a "very dignified and lovely man" after meeting him in Quebec shortly after the relief of the siege there.[2] That same officer also discussed how representatives of the Sioux Nation went aboard the *Isis* for breakfast the day after an audience with Sir Guy Carleton, and were impressed by Commodore Douglas and his warship.

---

[1] The song can be heard at All Songs Considered at *NPR.org*. Internet: http://www.npr.org/templates/story/story.php?storyId=18882029.

[2] Julius Friedrich von Hille and Helga Doblin (translator), *The American Revolution, Garrison Life in French Canada and New York: Journal of an Officer in the Prinz Fredrich Regiment, 1776-1783* (Westport, CT: Greenwood Press, 1993), p. 32.

But whatever fame and good will he garnered on both sides of the Atlantic in his time has all but faded over the decades, and he is now virtually unknown to everyone except experts in naval history or the American Revolution. Perhaps modern readers will feel the way one author did in a memoir published in *Gentleman's and London Magazine* two years after his death, when he wrote:

> The memoirs of this truly great and brave man, whether we regard his nautical skill and conduct as an experienced captain, or his gallantry as an enterprising, diligent, and intrepid officer; or whether we admire his assiduous humanity to those under his immediate command; will probably prove very interesting to the public at large, and peculiarly acceptable to that honourable profession to which Sir Charles Douglas was a conspicuous ornament. [1]

---

[1] "Memoirs of Sir Charles Douglas," *The Gentleman's and London Magazine: or Monthly Chronologer*, April, 1791 (London), p. 169.

CHAPTER TWO

EARLY LIFE AND THE SEVEN YEARS' WAR

In viewing the life of the late Sir Charles Douglas, your Lordships will find it a life of bustle and adventure.

Lord Chancellor Larborough[1]

Most articles on Sir Charles Douglas state that little is known of his early life, and it is true that information prior to the Seven Years War is difficult to obtain. Ironically, much of what *is* known about his early life and career is a result of the lawsuit his daughter, Lydia, and her husband, Reverend Richard Bingham, filed to obtain part of his estate. The suit involved the question of whether Douglas was a resident of England or Scotland at the time of his death, and as a result it was necessary for the judges in the case to outline his life and career.

Nearly every biographical entry on Sir Charles Douglas omits a birth date, and those that do not almost invariably estimate it to be 1834. However, his grave states his birth year as 1727, which coincides with numerous stories of him entering the navy in 1740 at age twelve. Douglas' parents were Charles Ayton Douglas and Christian Hepburn, both of Kinglassie, Fifeshire, Scotland, which is where some sources state he was born, although others say he was born in Perthshire. Charles Ayton Douglas was a medical doc-

---

[1] Paton, p. 457.

II

tor, and the family was somewhat wealthy because *his* father, William Ayton Douglas (also a doctor), had married the heiress to the estates of the Ayton family of Kinglassie and adopted the Ayton name. William's father, also named William, was heir to the title and lands of Douglas of Kirkness, which was handed down from his grandfather, Sir George Douglas of Kirkness, the son of William Douglas of Lochleven, 5th (or 6th) Earl of Morton.[1] Sir Charles was also a direct descendant of King James II of Scotland through Sir George's mother, Agnes Leslie. Nearly every account of Douglas' life mentions that he was related to the Earls of Morton, although very few mention his specific lineage. The reason this is considered noteworthy is that Earls rank third in precedence among the British peerage, after Dukes and Marquesses, and before Viscounts and Barons.

Douglas became wealthy himself through an inheritance from a relative, Ann Howard, Viscountess Irwin, who left him £9,000 upon her death in 1764. Lady Irwin's second husband was Major-General William Douglas, a close relative, and Charles once accidentally left a letter for some other, less fortunate relatives at their house that contained most of the prize money he had obtained as a midshipman. This impressed Lady Irwin so much that she became his patroness until her death. Douglas named his youngest daughter, Ann Irwin, of whom he was said to have been particularly fond, in her honor.

Some sources, including Debrett's Baronetage of 1840, state that both of his older brothers, William Ayton and Robert, died without male issue, leaving Charles as the representative of his line from the Earls of Morton. However, a letter to Helena in 1786 mentions a nephew whom he calls "Charles of Venlo" (presumably to distinguish the boy from himself and his own son Charles), the son of one of his older brothers who died in the Dutch service. It was almost certainly the second brother, Robert, who joined the service, since his oldest brother, William Ayton, had become heir to the Kirkness title in 1747 as well as that of Kinglassie upon his

---

[1] Sir John Bernard Burke, *Burke's Peerage, Baronetage, and Knightage,* 96th Edition (London: Shaw Publishing, 1938). Not paginated. There is a dispute over whether a previous holder of the Earldom was legitimate, so the numbering of the Earls changes depending on the source. Interestingly, Sir William of Lochleven and Agnes Leslie are direct ancestors of both Princess Diana and Camilla Parker-Bowles.

father's death in 1744.[1] In addition to his two older brothers and his sister Helena, Charles had three more brothers, John, James, and Sholto, and another sister, Jean.

Since Charles was not the oldest son, he followed in the tradition of many younger sons of aristocratic families in Britain and joined the service. In 1740, at the age of twelve, he entered the Royal Navy. While still a young man, he left to serve in the Dutch navy for three or four years, a fact that is often disputed but is set forth in legal documents for the succession case and other sources.[2] His service in a foreign navy prolonged the time it would take for him to be promoted in the navy of his homeland, and because of this he was not made a captain at as young an age as someone such as Rodney (who became a captain at age 23) or Nelson (who made post-captain at age 20).[3]

At the time of the first Siege of Louisbourg during King George's War in 1745, he was a midshipman in the British Royal Navy, serving in Commodore Warren's squadron. He also participated in the taking of Cape Breton. In 1747, he was serving as an interpreter for Admiral George Anson in the action with De la Jonquiere. It was then that he met De Grasse for the first time when the Frenchman, then an ensign, was captured with his ship.[4] He also passed the lieutenant's exam in 1747 and in 1748 served aboard the *Invincible*, 74 guns, under Sir Peter Warren.

Douglas certainly had some political connections, and his captain mentioned in a 1755 letter that Lord Morton knew him well. But according to N.A.M. Rodger, political connections were only helpful *in addition* to skill, and usually not enough for promotions

---

[1] *Burke's Peerage and Baronetage* (1938).

[2] David Robertson, *A Treatise on the Rules of the Law of Personal Succession* (Edinburgh: Thomas Clark, Law Bookseller, 1836), Appendix, p. 649.

[3] *The Naval Chronicle for 1805* (London: I. Gold, 1805), p. 443 (footnote). All following dates of Douglas' promotions are also confirmed by this source.

[4] Rear Admiral S.S. Robison, *History of Naval Tactics from 1530 to 1930: The Evolution of Tactical Maxims* (Annapolis, MD: The United States Naval Institute, 1942), p. 347.

on their own (the case of Rodney making his teenaged son a captain being one of those rare exceptions that proves the rule).[1]

Following the Peace of Aix-la-Chapelle between England, France, and Spain, Douglas decided that, rather than take the chance of being sent ashore, he would join a foreign navy. With the assistance of his patroness, the Lady Viscountess Irwin (the wife of his relative, then-Colonel William Douglas), he was able to become an officer in the Dutch Navy through none other than the Prince of Wales. In January 1749 he was made a lieutenant by the Admiralty of Amsterdam, and subsequently voyaged to such places as Lisbon and Cadiz. Not only did he increase his knowledge of seamanship and the world, he also learned more languages and improved his French, a skill that would serve him well throughout his career.

After returning to the British Navy, he was promoted to the rank of lieutenant on 4 December 1753.[2] Once Douglas was an officer, he rose swiftly through the ranks: Within six years of becoming a lieutenant, on 24 February 1759, he was promoted to commander, and was commanding HMS *Boscawen,* 16 guns, under Vice-Admiral Charles Saunders in the Quebec campaign of the Seven Years' War. According to John Knox Laughton, editor of the *Barham Papers,* Douglas was attached to Admiral Saunders' staff because he was an "excellent French scholar," something Rodney probably took into consideration years later when he made him captain of the fleet.[3] One of his duties was to procure French pilots to take Saunders and General Wolfe up the St. Lawrence River to Quebec. The Admiralty fitted out a cutter called the *Rodney* to quickly cross the Atlantic with Douglas and the pilots, but due to extremely difficult weather and the poor condition of the vessel, the decks were flooded during the entire journey. This caused Douglas to become gravely ill, and to lose the use of his left arm for the rest of his life.

But Douglas proved to be a valuable asset to his commanders. Because Montcalm believed the St. Lawrence to be unnavigable by

---

[1] N.A.M. Rodger, "Commissioned Officers' Careers in the Royal Navy, 1690-1815," *Journal for Maritime Research* (June 2001). Internet: http://www.jmr.nmm.ac.uk/server?show=ConJmrArticle.52&setPaginat e=No; N.A.M. Rodger, *The Wooden World* (New York: W.W. Norton & Company, 1986), p. 336.

[2] James Phinney Baxter, *The British Invasion from the North: The Campaigns of Generals Carleton and Burgoyne* (Albany, NY: Joel Munsell's Sons, 1887), p. 104.

[3] Laughton p. 179.

ships of the line, he was surprised to see the British ships arrive at Quebec City—a factor that helped the British defeat the French and take the city, and thus control of Canada. This would not be the last time Douglas would be instrumental in surprising an enemy by appearing on the St. Lawrence outside of Quebec City.

Douglas was made post-captain only two years later, on 13 March 1761, while commanding HMS *Unicorn*, 28 guns. The rank of post-captain of the time was the equivalent of a modern captain, but the distinction was made because any officer who commanded a ship was called "Captain," even if his rank was only that of commander or even lieutenant. But in order to command a ship of 6th rate or above, it was necessary to officially hold the rank of post-captain. Around this time, the Admiralty once again took notice of him when he came under fire by a superior French force, and rather than use typical British bludgeoning tactics, he decided to "cut as much as could be of his rigging with one broadside pointed high on purpose."[1] This may very well have been the action that won him his promotion.

The thing Douglas was most known for prior to the American Revolution was the part he played in repelling the French attack on St. John's, generally considered the final action of the French and Indian War (the American theater of the Seven Years' War). After serving for a time at the West India station commanding the sixth-rate *Syren*, 20 guns, he was transferred to the Newfoundland Station. While at Aquaforte in late June of 1762, the commanding officer at St. John's relayed the news of the French attack to him. Douglas sent all of his marines with their officer to St. John's to reinforce the garrison and help contain the situation. Before he left, he dispatched a small ship to the Banks to watch for Captain Graves on the *Antelope* and give him the intelligence.

Then Douglas sailed for Halifax and, on 2 July, reported the capture of St. John's to Commodore (later Rear-Admiral of the White) Lord Colville, who sent him back to his station to gather further intelligence. Next, Douglas supervised the repairs of the fortifications on the Isle of Boys.[2] When Lt.-Colonel William Amherst (sent by his older brother, Lord Amherst) landed at Torbay on 13 September 1762 to recapture the fort, Douglas commanded the covering naval force, and Amherst sent the signal for the land-

---

[1] Letter from Douglas to P. Durell, quoted in N.A.M. Rodger, *The Wooden World,* pp. 56-57.

[2] Lewis Amadeus Anspach, *A History of the Island of Newfoundland* (London: T. and J. Allman, 1819), p. 161.

ing from the *Syren*. Following the Battle of Signal Hill, the French capitulated on 18 September, and their navy slipped off during a storm at night. Douglas accorded himself so well in that action that he was chosen to transport Colville's dispatches to London the following month, and received a gift of £500 upon arriving at the Court of St. James' to report the news. [1]

After the Seven Years' War, the Treaty of Paris specified that England would give to France two islands off the entrance to Fortune Bay, called St. Pierre and Miquelon. Before the English were willing to give up the islands, they sent the now-legendary Captain James Cook aboard Douglas' next ship, the *Tweed*, 32 guns, to survey them. If the islands were going to fall into the hands of their historical enemy, the British wanted them fully mapped for strategic advantage in the future. While Cook was performing this task, the new French governor of the islands, Monsieur d'Anjac, along with some soldiers and settlers, arrived to take possession of them on the set date of 10 June 1763. Because Cook needed more time, it fell upon Captain Douglas to stall the governor. He convinced the French to remain on their ship until his superior officer, Captain Graves, could formally make the transition—not just briefly, but all the way until 4 July.

Then, after d'Anjac and the others disembarked at St. Pierre, Douglas somehow continued to stall them while Cook surveyed Miquelon until early in August. It is not recorded how Douglas was able to accomplish this, but he did write to the Admiralty afterwards asking for a payment of £50 "for the extraordinary expense I was put to." [2] The Admiralty was only too happy to pay.

In 1764, Douglas became a flag officer in the Russian Navy, once again as a result of high-level influence in London in the form of his patroness, the Lady Viscountess Irwin. The Russian ambassador had previously requested the assistance of a Royal Navy captain, two lieutenants, and two midshipmen (each of whom would raise one step in rank in Russia) on behalf of Catherine the Great. When Douglas was chosen, he resigned his commission in the British Navy in March of that year, with the permission of the

---

[1] Douglas, W.A.B. "Sir Charles Douglas," *Dictionary of Canadian Biography Online*. Internet: http://www.biographi.ca/en/ShowBio.asp?BioId=35982&query

[2] John Noble Wilford, *The Mapmakers: Revised Edition*. New York: Vintage Books, a division of Random House (2000) pp. 172-174; Arthur Kitson, *The Life of Captain James Cook*, Kila, MT: Kessinger Publishing (2004) p. 54.

King, which was given to him via the Princess of Wales. Douglas helped the Empress to reorganize her fleet as a rear admiral, along with the man he chose as his second in command, fellow Scotsman Lt. Sir Samuel Greig, who became a captain. They conducted the campaign of the summer of 1764 aboard the *St. Dometrie Rofstofskoi*, a triple-decker captained by Greig.

Douglas returned to England through Holland in January 1765 to move his family to Russia via Scotland as soon as conditions on the Baltic Sea would allow. However, upon his arrival in London, he received a document from the Russian minister that he felt compromised his allegiance to Great Britain, namely an order from the Admiralty in St. Petersburg to recruit British workers to help build Russian ships. Because this was something that went against the conditions of his service under the Empress, Douglas resigned immediately, leaving Samuel Greig in charge of the fledgling navy. Greig would spend twenty-five years there and later became known as the creator of the Russian Navy and one of its greatest admirals. Many years later, after Greig's death, Catherine tried to lure Douglas back again, but he had become a rear admiral with the British, and she was unsuccessful then as well.[1]

The fact that Douglas remained employed by the Royal Navy during the inter-war years while so many others were set ashore with half pay is yet another acknowledgment of his abilities and value to the Admiralty. He was given command of HMS *Emerald*, 32 guns, a frigate that served as a cruiser off the Scottish Station, in 1767. The post lasted the traditional three years. Even when there were no military objectives to keep him busy, Douglas managed to find other ways to occupy his mind. In 1769, he sent an article to the Royal Society entitled, "An Account of the Result of Some Attempts Made to Ascertain the Temperature of the Sea in Great Depths, Near the Coasts of Lapland and Norway; as Also Some Anecdotes, Collected in the Former," which was published the next year in the Society's *Philosophical Transactions* journal. As the title indicates, it consisted mostly of measurements of the temperature of seawater near Lapland and Norway, taken at different depths using various techniques. He described in detail how he improved his methods to get the thermometer down near the ocean floor faster and bring it back up as quickly as possible—admittedly not very exciting for a modern reader. However, the an-

---

[1] Anthony Cross, *By the Banks of the Neva: Chapters from the Lives and Careers of the British in Eighteenth-Cenury Russia* (Cambridge: Cambridge University Press, 1997), pp. 184, 204.

ecdotal stories he added to the article are definitely quite interesting, especially his hunt for the legendary Kraaken (or Kraken), a gigantic squid or octopus, which he determined was probably a myth and "whose dimensions...appear to me to be far beyond the scale of nature."[1] He also searched for evidence of the Stoor Worm, or Sea Worm, which was supposedly a giant sea serpent with a long neck and tale, similar to the legendary Loch Ness Monster. Following his investigation, Douglas believed the creature was real thanks to a story from a seemingly reliable source. Finally, he attempted to learn a scientific cause for the whirlpool, or maal stroom, which he said was located between the islands of Lofoot. After giving an account of an explanation by a Norwegian man, he felt that he had some grasp of how it was happening, but still felt that his understanding of the phenomenon was imperfect.

Not mentioned in the article is Douglas' 1769 voyage to the northern coast of Lapland with two astronomers to attempt to observe the transit of Venus. The trip proved unsuccessful, as the weather was too overcast for such an experiment to work.

In 1770 Douglas was appointed to HMS *St. Albans*, 64 guns, and sent to the Windward Islands station, as the British were dealing with a conflict with Spain over the Falkland Islands at that time. After that conflict was resolved, the *St. Albans* served as a guard ship at the home station until 1773.[2] For the remainder of 1773 and throughout 1774, Douglas was appointed to the *Ardent*, also 64 guns, which served as a guard ship in the Medway.

If Charles Douglas had retired or been killed in action during this part of his life, he would already have left behind an interesting and honorable career as a naval officer. However, the most significant part of his life was yet to come, during the War of American Independence.

---

[1] Charles Douglas, "An Account of the Result of Some Attempts Made to Ascertain the Temperature of the Sea in Great Depths, Near the Coasts of Lapland and Norway; as Also Some Anecdotes, Collected in the Former. By Charles Douglas Esquire, F.R.S. Then Captain of His Majesty's Ship the Emerald, Anno 1769, *Philosophical Transactions (1683-1775)*, Vol. 60 (London: The Royal Society), pp. 39-45. Internet: accessed through JSTOR at http://www.jstor.org/stable/105875.

[2] Charnock, p. 427.

CHAPTER THREE
THE RELIEF OF QUEBEC

For God's sake, get the *Isis* down to Blackstakes....

Your being able to leave early in February is of the utmost importance to the public service. I think the fate of Quebec depends upon it.

> John Montagu, Lord Sandwich,
> First Lord of the Admiralty,
> to Captain Charles Douglas[1]

Many turning points in the American Revolution have been cited by historians as being essential to the eventual outcome of the war, and it is quite common to read discussions of what might have been had the Americans lost certain battles, or if a particular person had not been where he was at a certain moment. It is far more rare to read about what might have happened in the other direction; in other words, what if the Americans had accomplished *more* during that fateful war? One example of this would be the failed invasion of Quebec, in which Colonel Benedict Arnold and General Richard Montgomery led men into Canada at separate points, and then converged on Quebec. What might have been if Montgomery hadn't been killed, or if rebel reinforcements had ar-

---

[1] Lt. James M. Hadden, *Hadden's Journal and Orderly Books: a Journal Kept in Canada and Upon Burgoyne's Campaign in 1776 and 1777* (Albany, NY: Joel Munsell's Sons, 1884), p. 296 (footnote).

rived before the British relief effort? It is impossible to know for certain, but one can certainly speculate that the Province of Quebec would have been the fourteenth colony in rebellion, and Canada may have become part of the new United States. The possible scenarios to be extracted from such a theoretical outcome are staggering. If America had acquired the vast territory that is now Canada, it would have made the Louisiana Purchase pale in comparison—perhaps even made it unnecessary. And what about the War with Mexico to acquire land in the American Southwest?

Yet the fact remains that the American rebels were not able to capture Canada in 1776, because on 6 May of that year, their siege of Quebec City was lifted when a squadron of Royal Navy ships commanded by Captain Charles Douglas arrived on the St. Lawrence River and literally sent the rebels running.

At the start of the American Revolution in 1775, Captain Charles Douglas was at home in Gosport with his second wife, Sarah Wood (his famous son, General Sir Howard Douglas was born on 23 January 1776). He had been commander of HMS *Ardent*, 61 guns, at the home station for two years, but the situation in America soon changed that. The 11 November 1775 issue of *The London Chronicle* printed an "Extract of a Letter from Gosport, Nov. 9," in which it mistakenly called him "John Douglas, esq," and stated that he was "appointed to the command of his Majesty's ship *Isis*, of 50 guns, and will go to America shortly, as third in command; Admiral Shuldham being first, and Sir Peter Parker second in command." [1] As fate would have it, this was but one day after Arnold and his men had arrived at Point Levi, across the river from Quebec City, and began to prepare for their attack.

Arnold's march, which led to the nickname "the American Hannibal," began in Massachusetts with about 1100 men, continued up through the treacherous Maine wilderness, and ended outside of Quebec City, where he met up with a small army led by General Richard Montgomery. They placed the city under siege, but American mortar fire had little effect on the strong walls around the city. With many of their soldiers' commissions about to expire at the end of the year, Montgomery and Arnold decided to attack during blizzard conditions on 31 December. The attack, which also included such men as Daniel Morgan and Aaron Burr, failed, with Montgomery killed and Arnold wounded in the leg.

---

[1] William Bell Clark (ed.), *Naval Documents of the American Revolution, Vol. 3* (Washington: U.S. Government Printing Office 1968) p. 356.

Arnold, who was promoted to brigadier general, continued to command the siege from his bed, and remained in charge of that Continental force until April, when he was relieved by General Wooster.

By the middle of January, Lord Sandwich, First Lord of the Admiralty, was hoping that the *Isis* would lead a small squadron, including the frigate *Surprise* (commanded by Captain Robert Linzee) and the sloop *Martin* (commanded by Captain Henry Harvey), all full of troops and supplies, across the Atlantic in early February. Quebec had been under siege for weeks by then, and the King and Lord George Germain, Secretary of State for the Colonies, were pushing him to get the first wave of troops and ships over there as soon as possible.

Another *London Chronicle* article, dated 13 January 1776, indicated that *Isis* was "ready for sailing to America, and only waits a fair wind."[1] A third article, dated February 3 to 6, described a letter from Chatham on February 1st that stated, "This day a detachment of marines, consisting of one captain, one lieutenant, two serjeants [sic], two corporals, one drummer, and 49 private men, embarked hence on board his Majesty's ship *Isis*, of 50 guns, at this port, commanded by Charles Douglas, Esq; bound for America."[2] The same paper announced that it would be Lord Richard Howe, not Admiral Shuldham, who would be first in command of the Royal Navy in America. The next issue, dated 10-13 February 1776, told of the *Isis* leaving for Blackstakes on 7 February, "to take in her powder and guns, after which she is to proceed without the least loss of time."

It was at this time that Douglas received from the Admiralty his orders for the expedition, which were very specific:

Whereas Lord George Germaine [sic] One of His Majesty's principal Secretaries of State, has acquainted Us...that it is the King's intention that every effort be made to send relief to Quebec, And whereas we intend that the Ship you command shall take on board one Captain, one Lieutenant one Ensign & Ninety four private Men part of the 29th Regiment doing duty at Chatham & proceed on this Service, You are therefore, after having embarked the said Troops which you are to bear on a Supernumerary List for Victuals

---

[1] Clark, *Vol. 3*, p. 491.

[2] *Ibid*, p. 882.

at two thirds allowance, hereby required & directed to put to Sea without loss of time; And...make the best of your way to the Isle of aux Coudres in the River St Lawrence, observing if upon entering the Gulph [sic] of St Lawrence you find the passage through it impracticable on account of the Ice, to make the nearest & safest Port, watching with great attention the earliest opportunity of proceeding upon your Voyage. [1]

Once he reached Canada, he was to immediately ascertain from the inhabitants whether Quebec was still in British hands, and, if so, find a way to let Governor Carleton know he was on his way and ask how he could best assist him. If he found that the rebels had taken the town, he was to remain at Isle aux Coudres, disembark the troops, and wait until reinforcements arrived. The orders then detailed how Douglas should proceed under a number of different scenarios. He was also to put any ships commanded by officers junior to him under his command, discover if any enemy ships were cruising the St. Lawrence River, and await further instructions from Vice Admiral Shuldham, or whomever the commanding naval officer in North America might be at that time (which is odd, considering the orders are dated 16 February, and a newspaper article of two weeks earlier announced that Howe was replacing Shuldham).[2] In some areas, Douglas was given a great deal of discretion, while in others he would find very little leeway accorded him.

Along with the 29th Regiment, which would serve under Major-General John Burgoyne after he arrived a few weeks later, the squadron also carried a letter from Lord Germain to Governor Sir Guy Carleton with orders on how to proceed and information on a second wave of troops to follow. However, it was assumed that the first wave, along with the marines, sailors, and other support from the men-of-war, would be enough to break the siege unless the Americans had already taken the city. The second wave was primarily to be an invasion force eventually bound for America.

Another *London Chronicle* article announced that the *Isis* was finally leaving St. Helen's for Quebec—on 7 March 1776, about a

---

[1] *Ibid*, p. 912.
[2] *Ibid*, p. 913.

month later than Lord Sandwich had wanted.[1] But a later letter from Douglas indicated that they left Portland on 11 March, so the delays actually continued for several more days. According to other letters at the time, including one written by Lord Cornwallis dated 7 March, the winds were blowing very strongly in the wrong direction, and a *Chronicle* announcement told of a ship having to come back to port on 6 March as a result. Nevertheless, things turned around after that date, and Douglas made the transatlantic trip in only about four weeks.

Despite the desperate order of the Admiralty, those who knew Canada did not believe Captain Douglas had any chance of reaching Quebec City in time to relieve the siege. The French ambassador in London, Count de Guines, wrote to the French Foreign Minister, Count de Vergennes, in February:

> Consequently they have ordered an embarkation of a reinforcement of eight hundred men that M. [Charles] Douglas, an experienced sea officer, believes he can take into the St. Lawrence River in early April. To tell the truth, all the facts are against any hope of success in such an undertaking; every single man who knows Quebec and the river declares that it is impossible to sail there with a squadron before the first days of May; however, M. Douglas insists on taking this responsibility.[2]

As expected, when the squadron reached the Gulf of St. Lawrence, it was packed with ice ten-to-twelve feet thick. In a letter to Secretary of the Admiralty Philip Stephens dated 8 May 1776, Captain Douglas described the ordeal of making his way into and up the St. Lawrence River. He first stated that they reached the Island of St. Peters on 11 April, exactly a month after leaving Portland. Once they got underway, it was mostly smooth sailing, and they were able to make the crossing in extremely good time. When they encountered the field of ice, Douglas tried several winding courses into the Gulf of St. Lawrence, to no avail. "We then," he wrote...

> ...with a velocity of about 5 knots tried to what effect, the running down a large piece of Ice, of about 10 or 12 feet thickness, would have upon the Ship, and she ran it to pieces. Encouraged by this experiment, we thought it an enterprize, worthy of an English ship of the line, in our King and Country's sacred cause, and an effort due to the

---

[1] *Ibid*, p. 949.
[2] *Ibid*, p. 914.

gallant defenders of Quebec, to make the attempt of pressing her by force of Sail, thro' the thick, broad and closely connected fields of Ice (as formidable as the gulph [sic] of St Lawrence ever exhibited) to which we saw no bounds towards the Western part of our horizon, and we shaped our Course accordingly.[1]

It was certainly not an obvious choice to ram the ice. As author Michael Pearson points out, Douglas tested the maneuver, "Courageously, for it was the type of operation that could be costly to a career officer in the navy should he be wrong..."[2] They proceeded for another eight leagues in such a manner "with bits of the sheathing off the Ships bottom; and sometimes pieces of the Cutwater, but none of the Oak Plank," until a snowstorm forced them to stop for the night. They continued on using this method, and at times Lord Petersham would exercise his troops out on "the Crusted surface of that fluid" as they were stopped. Douglas continued:

> After 9 days of unspeakable Toil for 50, or 60 Leagues, & having put in Practise various expedients, too manifold to particularize, some of more, some of less efficacy in Order to fortify the Ships bows, against the continual friction, or strokes of the Ice, and to break or remove it, from before her. On the 21st April we got clear of it, made the Island of Anticosti and that evening entered the River St Lawrence, in a Snow Storm.[3]

By the 30th, they were near the Pilgrims and on 3 May they anchored near the Isle aux Coudres. Both the *Surprise* and the *Martin*, faster ships than the *Isis*, joined them, and they secured all the Canadian pilots they could there. On the 5th, Douglas ordered Captain Linzee of the *Surprise*, the fastest of the ships and "a remarkably good sailor," to move ahead and let the city know they were on their way. All three ships arrived early the next morning, on 6 May 1776, a mere seven weeks after leaving England.

Most versions of the squadron's arrival would have one believe that as soon as the first ship rounded the bend around dawn, the entire city recognized it as their salvation and prepared a great

---

[1] *Ibid*, p. 1451.

[2] Michael Pearson, *Those Damned Rebels: The American Revolution as Seen Through British Eyes*, (Cambridge, MA: Da Capo Press, 1972), p. 150.

[3] Clark, *Vol. 4*, p. 1451.

welcome. However, the diary of an unnamed artillery officer stationed on the walls of Quebec during the siege gives a first-hand account of the appropriately named *Surprise*'s arrival and indicates that there was some tension before the celebrating began.

> About day light a Ship appeared below Point Levy—The Drums immediately beat to Arms & the Alarm bell rung, which in a few minutes brought the whole Garrison to the Grand Parade, save the Gunners who manned the different Batteries, as soon as She came in full view of the town We fired across her from the grand Battery; She instantly fired three Guns to Leeward & hoisted our Signal, then bore away & anchored before the town—it proved to be the Surprise frigate, Capt. Lindsay, & shortly after the Merlin Sloop & Isis, Sr. C: Douglas arrived—they brought part of the 29 Regt. & a few Marines who were landed directly, & so soon as the Men had eat a little& rested about an hour, all the Garrison were ordered under Arms to go out with the General to the plains of Abraham. [1]

Other sources say the firing of the guns was a prearranged signal (some claiming the *Surprise* fired seven guns). Regardless, the entire city soon became aware that they were being saved from their besiegers. Nearly every account describes the elation of the people of Quebec upon hearing the news that British reinforcements had arrived, as well as the shock and panic of the American besiegers. The journal of one American, Dr. Isaac Senter, said their troops took flight "in the most irregular, *helter skelter* manner."[2] Captain Douglas described the rebel reaction in his own colorful way, starting with those manning the battery on Point Levi:

> Aw'd by our run out cannon theirs, tho on an eminence observed a profound Silence; and the Rebel Troops, who served them seemed to gaze with astonishment, at our Landing our several detachments, At one o'clock, his Excellency General Carleton, wisely availing himself of the very different impressions our arrival had made on the Minds of the Rebels, and of his valorous Garrison, marched out at the head of about 800 Men, and Swept, or rather frightened away the panic struck Multitude: consisting of about

---

[1] Fred C. Würtele (ed.), *Blockade of Quebec in 1775-1776 by the American Revolutionists*, (Port Washington, NY: Kennikat Press, 1970), p. 51.

[2] Quoted in James Kirby Martin, *Benedict Arnold, Revolutionary Hero: An American Warrior Reconsidered* (New York: New York University Press, 1997), p. 209.

3000 Men at least, (now for the first time exposed to their very Buckles) from the celebrated height of Abraham where instead of teasing, they were just beginning to break ground in good earnest before the Capital of Canada.[1]

After the British soldiers began routing the rebels, Douglas sent the *Surprise*, the *Martin*, and a vessel that had already been at Quebec, "with orders to annoy their retreat, to take or destroy their Craft on the Water, & intercept any Stores or cannon expected from Montreal." He called the rebel retreat "a flight perhaps the most precipitate ever heard of: for they left not only their undischarged Cannon, ammunition, scaling ladders, intrenching [sic] tools, and provisions: but even many of them their Muskets; & every other sort of encumbrance." He then relayed stories told to the British by captured American soldiers of their officers taking off on horseback as soon as they heard the news of the ships, leaving their men behind.

Douglas finished his letter by telling Stephens about the excellent service of certain other officers (who "would have done honor to ancient Greece, or Rome in their more virtuous days"), and congratulating the Admiralty "on the returning prosperity, of the loyal Cause, & the utter ruin of the rebellious one in Canada, (the existence whereof wholly depended on the taking of Quebec)."[2] Of the ensuing advance of the British forces, a British naval officer under Douglas who found a lot to criticize about other commanders repeatedly emphasized the excellent tactical decisions of Douglas.

Now a Brigadier General, Benedict Arnold, who was in Montreal at the time of Douglas' arrival, was still holding out hope of reinforcements on 8 May, two days before he learned of the relief of Quebec. In a letter to General Washington dated that day, he wrote, "I hope we shall be able to Maintain these two Posts [on the St. Lawrence] until a reinforcement Arrives to our Assistance, which we are told are on their way here. These are the only Posts that secure the River, until you approach near Montreal and of so much consequence, that Nothing but superiour [sic] numbers will oblige us to abandon them."[3] The same day, he wrote another letter to Major General Thomas, who had just taken command of the siege of Quebec from General Wooster, in which he offered his

---

[1] Clark, *Vol. 4*, p. 1451.

[2] *Ibid*, p. 1451.

[3] *Ibid*, p. 1456.

congratulations to him "on the prospect of reinforcements arriving, soon."[1] In fact, over two thousand troops were on their way from New York City under Brigadier General William Thompson, and had been since April.

But it was too late. The Americans did abandon their posts, and eventually all of Canada, once Douglas' squadron, as well as some troops sent by General Sir William Howe, had arrived. In fact, it was Arnold himself who became the last uncaptured Continental soldier to leave Canadian soil at the end of the retreat over a month later.[2] From the correspondence of Arnold and others, it is apparent that the Americans felt that all they needed was a little more time, some supplies and reinforcements, and they would be able to take Quebec. But it was not to be, thanks to Captain Douglas' daring experiment in ramming the ice and coming up the river weeks earlier than anyone could have reasonably expected, or hoped for.

There was no rest for Charles Douglas after doing his part to save Canada from American control. Little did he know at the time that his next task would push his resourcefulness to the limit. His reward for the relief of Quebec, in addition to a Commodore's pennant, was to be put in charge of assembling a fleet of ships from scratch to destroy the small navy being built by Benedict Arnold. As noted by A.T. Mahan, "The Navy had once again decided the fate of Canada, and was soon also to determine that of Lake Champlain."[3]

---

[1] *Id.*

[2] James L. Nelson, *Benedict Arnold's Navy* (Camden, Maine: International Marine/McGraw Hill 2006), p. 217.

[3] A.T. Mahan, *Major Operations of the Navies in the War of American Independence* (Gloucestershire, UK: Nonsuch Publishing Ltd, 2006), p. 18.

CHAPTER FOUR

THE BATTLE OF VALCOUR ISLAND

It was a strife of pigmies for the prize of a continent...

Alfred Thayer Mahan[1]

The Battle of Valcour Island on Lake Champlain is often cited as the reason the British army was unable to invade the fledgling United States from Canada in 1776. In fact, it can be argued that, had that battle not slowed down the British and convinced Sir Guy Carleton to wait until after the winter to invade, they most likely would have taken New York, effectively cutting off New England from the rest of the country and possibly ending the war very early on. While most historians would agree with this assessment, the battle is often underplayed and under appreciated as a major turning point in the American Revolution. As an example, in *For the Common Defense*, a popular military history of the United States by Allan Millett and Peter Maslowski, the battle receives but three sentences in the large section on the American Revolution.[2] Even worse, some books on the war do not even mention the battle at all.

---

[1] Mahan, *Major Operations*, p. 22.

[2] Allan R. Millet and Peter Maslowski, *For the Common Defense: A Military History of the United States of America* (New York: The Free Press, 1994), p. 69.

Other historians, however, recognize its great importance. In his essay in *What if? The World's Foremost Military Historians Imagine What Might Have Been*, Thomas Fleming lists the absence of the Battle of Valcour Island as one of the ways the Americans could have lost the Revolution. Under the subheading "What if General Benedict Arnold had not turned himself into Admiral Arnold on Lake Champlain?" Fleming states, "If Brigadier General Benedict Arnold had lacked the nautical know-how—and incredible nerve—to launch an American fleet on Lake Champlain in the late summer of 1776, the British would have wintered in Albany and been ready to launch a war of annihilation against New England in the spring of 1777."[1] Fleming continues to posit that Carleton would have had the ability to demolish New England from the undefended West in much the same way Sherman marched through the South during the Civil War. Robert Leckie simply states in *George Washington's War* that "In his valorous delaying action at Valcour Island, 'Admiral' Arnold had saved the Revolution."[2]

Many experts even go so far as to consider the Battle of Valcour Island the only meaningful American naval battle of the war. It is the only battle fought by the Americans that is mentioned by Alfred Thayer Mahan in *The Major Operations of the Navies in the War of American Independence*. William M. Fowler, Jr., argues that the Continental navy "could never adequately defend either the coast or shipping. One notable exception to this, and perhaps the greatest American achievement afloat, was the trading of space for time that Benedict Arnold orchestrated on Lake Champlain."[3]

This "what if?" scenario can be analyzed in the other direction as well. If the British had not bothered to launch its small naval force on Lake Champlain, their virtually defenseless transports would have been easily destroyed by Arnold's small gunboats as they attempted to move the army south. Such a staggering defeat and loss of troops would have once again left Canada wide open

---

[1] Thomas Fleming, "Unlikely Victory: Thirteen Ways the Americans Could Have Lost the Revolution," *What if?The World's Foremost Military Historians Imagine What Might Have Been*, Cowley, Robert, editor (New York: Berkely Books, 1999), p. 166.

[2] Robert Leckie, *George Washington's War: The Saga of the American Revolution* (New York: Harper Perenial/Harper Collins, 1992), p. 306.

[3] Fowler, p. 263.

for invasion, and the British might have lost fourteen colonies instead of thirteen.

The part Benedict Arnold played in turning the previously disastrous project of building a small flotilla into a successful operation is very well documented in such books as *Benedict Arnold's Navy* by James Nelson. Sir Guy Carleton, who led the British in Canada, and Lieutenant Thomas Pringle, who commanded the small British navy on the lake, are major players in most descriptions of the battle. But what about Arnold's counterpart on the British side, whom eminent naval historian Kenneth Hagan calls "the officer most responsible for this British ascendancy?"[1] How was he able to assemble a force of so many ships, including a Ship of the Line, in so short a time, on a lake with no navigable access to the ocean or the St. Lawrence River?

Commodore Charles Douglas brought the same ingenuity he was already becoming famous for to the assembly of the fleet for Lake Champlain in 1776. John R. Bratten described the dilemma faced by Douglas:

> The British were faced with two choices: they could start from scratch and build a new fleet of ships at St. Jean, much as the Americans were doing at Skenesborough, or they could attempt to carry part of their existing force either through or around the St. Therese rapids between Chambly and St. Jean. Captain Charles Douglas, commander of the St. Lawrence fleet, believed the first choice would be a mistake. With the short time available to the British that summer, the best they could hope to build at St. Jean would be several small vessels. What Douglas believed the British really needed were a few large vessels, ones powerful enough to confront and overwhelm the weaker fleet the Americans were putting together....In the end the British decided to do both.[2]

Carpenters, riggers, sail makers, and caulkers were brought to Fort St. John's to build ships, as well as Canadian prisoners who would be forced to work. A. T. Mahan says, "A large fleet of transports and ships of war in the St. Lawrence supplied the British with adequate resources, which were utilized judiciously and ener-

---

[1] Kenneth J. Hagan, *This People's Navy: The Making of American Sea Power* (New York: The Free Press, 1991), p. 8.

[2] John R. Bratten, *The Gondola Philadelphia and the Battle of Lake Champlain,* (College Station: Texas A&M University Press, 2002), p. 38.

getically by Captain Douglas; but to get these to the Lake was a long and arduous task."[1] Hundreds of bateaux and over two dozen longboats were dragged twelve miles from Chambly up the rapids as far as possible, then put onto rollers and pulled by horses the rest of the way through the forest. But when this same feat was attempted with the two 12-gun schooners, the *Carleton* and the *Maria* (name for Carleton's wife), they turned out to be too heavy and actually started to destroy the road beneath them. Instead, the schooners were broken down and carried in pieces, then assembled on stocks at St. John's.

Douglas did whatever was necessary to get the ships built and fitted, stating, "We can only strain every nerve, in contributing as far as possible, towards the procurement thereof." As he wrote in a letter to Philip Stephens on 21 July 1776: "The Masters of the Ships, having done honor to their Country, by their Willingness during the whole course of this prosperous expedition, do not Scruple to return to England, without Long boats, (and I hope Carpenters too; at least such of them whose Ships are not leaky) on this important occasion."[2] Out of necessity, Douglas even borrowed the guns from his own ship, *Isis*, and other ships that would remain relatively safe on the St. Lawrence "'till the Lake Business be over."[3]

Douglas discovered a real prize in Quebec: a 180-ton ship was already in the process of being built there. He quickly commandeered the ship, then had it marked, broken down into pieces, and transported upriver to be finished at St. John's by dozens of carpenters. This ship-of-the-line would carry eighteen twelve-pound guns and come to be named *Inflexible*, "the prowess of which," in Douglas' own words, "will give us the dominion of Lake Champlain without a doubt." [4] Douglas ordered Lt. Schank of the *Canceaux* to take all of his men, supplies, stores, sails, and even anchors to be used on the *Inflexible*. Until the ship was finished, Schank became the superintendent of the shipyard, a job at which he excelled.

---

[1] Mahan, *Major Operations*, p. 21.

[2] Douglas to Philip Stephens, 21 July1776, William James Morgan, (ed.), *Naval Documents of the American Revolution*, vol. V. (Washington: U.S. Government Printing Office, 1972), p. 1167.

[3] Douglas to Lord Howe, 4 August 1776, in Morgan, pp. 43-43.

[4] Douglas to Captain Philemon Pownoll, R.N., 23 September 1776. Morgan, p. 951.

Many ships had to be taken apart down to the waterline in order to be moved up the rapids, including the captured American gondola called *Convert*, which was renamed either *Royal* or *Loyal Convert* (depending on the source). The "gondolo," as Douglas called it, "cuts a very good appearance and is to carry Six Nines and (in the bow) an Army 24 pounder."[1]

The manning of the vessels also fell to Commodore Douglas. He chose Lieutenant Thomas Pringle (who eventually became a Vice-Admiral) to be commander-in-chief of the fleet, along with six other officers for other vessels. Lieutenant (also later Vice-Admiral) James Richard Dacres was made commander of the *Carleton*, but was wounded during the battle. A young midshipman named Edward Pellew, who eventually became Vice-Admiral of the United Kingdom and Viscount Exmouth, took command and fought valiantly. An account of his heroic actions was sent by Douglas to Admiral Howe, who in turn sent a letter to Pellew promising him a lieutenant's commission when he reached New York.[2] Douglas and Captain Pownoll both mentioned Pellew's heroism in letters to Lord Sandwich at the Admiralty, and Sandwich was so impressed that he wrote to Pellew himself.[3]

To meet the need for seven hundred sailors, he used the crews of the *Isis* and the *Lizard*, as well as draftees from other British vessels. He offered increased pay to sailors who were willing to serve on Lake Champlain, in order to encourage them to volunteer.[4] This would turn out to be very beneficial in the battle, since almost none of the Americans were naval officers, and most of them not even true sailors, but rather soldiers with some experience at sea.

In mid-August, Douglas wrote to the Admiralty that the lake fleet would soon "cut a noble figure." A document entitled "Force on the Lake [Champlain] Tolerably Exact, on Septr 18th, 1776" lists the names, guns, and commanders of the small fleet. In addition to the *Inflexible*, the *Maria*, and the *Carleton,* there was a radeau (later christened *Thunderer*), the gondola *Royal Convert*, twenty-eight gunboats, four long boats, and twenty-six transport vessels,

---

[1] *Id.*

[2] *The Annual Biography and Obituary: 1834*, Vol. XVIII (London: Longman, Rees, Orme, Brown, Green, & Longman, 1834), p. 3.

[3] Edward Osler, *The Life of Admiral Viscount Exmouth* (London: Biblio-Bazaar, 2007, original copyright 1854), pp. 30-31.

[4] Douglas to Philip Stephens in Morgan, pp. 762-763.

along with over four hundred "batoes" (bateaux) for the convey-ance of the troops.[1] The gunboats had been built, for the most part, back in England, and then transported to Quebec in pieces. These each had one 24- to 9-pounder, and some of them had Howitzers. The flat-bottomed bateaux, otherwise known as King's Boats or Royal Boats, could each carry thirty to forty troops and had square bows for easy disembarkation. The *Thunderer*, the only vessel constructed completely at St. John's, was the most heavily armed vessel built. Basically a 91-foot raft, it served as a gun platform for six 24-pounders, six 12-pounders, and two Howitzers.[2]

Kenneth Hagan of the Naval War College states that Douglas "outclassed Arnold in three vital material categories: men, ships, and guns. Only in tactical judgment did the British prove inferior to the Americans." According to Hagan, the main reason the Brit-ish did not secure an easier, quicker victory was that Thomas Pringle, the naval officer who actually commanded the squadron on Lake Champlain, neglected to send a scouting party ahead. Had he done so, and the Americans had been detected before the Brit-ish sailed past them, then an even greater victory would surely have resulted.[3] Mahan is also extremely critical of Pringle's over-sight, calling it "a very serious blunder."[4]

Valcour Island is only between one half and three quarters of a mile from the western coast of Lake Champlain, and Arnold hid his small fleet there on 11 October, hoping to remain undetected while the British passed by. By the time the British did spot them, they were already downwind, and had serious difficulty moving back into firing range. As a consequence, they were not able to de-feat the inferior American force on the first day despite some heavy action, and drew anchor in a line across the southern open-ing of the strait between the island and the mainland. General John Burgoyne, who was at St. John's, wrote to Douglas the next morning and told him that, based on the intelligence he had ob-tained regarding the battle and the situation at nightfall, the Americans must have either surrendered or given them battle on their own terms by the time he was writing him that morning. However, this was not the case. Under cover of darkness and a

---

[1] Morgan, pp. 883-884.

[2] Bratten, p. 41.

[3] Hagan, p. 7.

[4] Mahan, *Major Operations*, p. 26.

heavy fog, Arnold slipped his flotilla past the British ships without detection. By the time the fog cleared the next morning (12 October) and the British realized what had happened and began the chase, the Americans were eight miles ahead. But Arnold's fleet was forced to anchor for repairs and the wind was now coming from the south, so the lead dwindled to five miles. On the 13th, a fresh breeze came in from the northeast for the British, and they soon caught up to Arnold and began pummeling his flotilla. The action went on for about two and a half hours, with most of the American boats being destroyed, and some of those that weren't being burned by their own crews once they reached shore to keep them out of the hands of the British. The last of the American forces, including Arnold himself, retreated on foot to Crown Point, where they burned their fortifications and moved on to Ticonderoga. American casualties exceeded eighty, while the British were less than forty.

Under better circumstances, Sir Guy Carleton may very well have decided to take Fort Ticonderoga at that time (an almost inevitable, if not easy, victory) and moved on to Albany as planned. Many historians believe it had been a mistake for Carleton to wait the extra four weeks for *Inflexible* to be finished, as it was probably not vital to the fleet's ability to defeat the rebels, and would have allowed plenty of time to take Ticonderoga and move on to Albany. Yet Douglas believed otherwise: "I scruple not to say, that had not General Carleton authorized me to take the extraordinary measure of sending up the *Inflexible* from Quebec, things could not this year have been brought to so glorious a conclusion on Lake Champlain."

Even with the actual outcome of the battle, it was still considered a great victory among the British, although those in Whitehall were quite disappointed that Carleton did not continue on.[1] Regardless, Carleton was made a Knight of the Bath thanks to the victory, and Douglas was made 1st Baronet of Carr. Further, Douglas sent a letter bragging of the victory to the British ambassador at Madrid, hoping to help their cause with regard to Spain. Notwithstanding the supposition involved following the battle, there is no doubt that both the Americans and the British put forth their full effort and did their countries proud on Lake Champlain. As Mahan stated following his listing of the vessels involved in the battle and their armament: "These minutiae are necessary for the proper appreciation of what Captain Douglas justly called a 'mo-

---

[1] Pearson, p. 231.

mentous event.' It was a strife of pigmies for the prize of a continent, and the leaders are entitled to full credit both for their antecedent energy and for their dispositions in the contest." [1]

---

[1] Mahan, *Major Operations*, p. 22.

CHAPTER FIVE

IN THE CHANNEL FLEET:
USHANT AND THE RELIEF
OF GIBRALTAR

I did not observe anything done or left undone by Admiral
Keppel, on the 27th or 28th of July, bearing the appearance
of his negligently performing his duty.

> Sir Charles Douglas
> at the court martial of
> Admiral Augustus Keppel[1]

After returning from Canada, Sir Charles Douglas was back at
the home station commanding the *Stirling Castle*, 64 guns. It was
apparently during this time that he was introduced to a young
lieutenant named Horatio Nelson by Captain Mark Robinson of
the *Worcester*. Although Sir Charles did not live to see Nelson become the greatest admiral in British history, his son, Sir William-
Henry Douglas, would be one of the few admirals given the honor
of carrying the canopy at Nelson's funeral.

---

[1] *The Trial of the Honourable Augustus Keppel, Admiral of the Blue
Squadron, at a Court Martial*, Recorded by Thomas Blandemor. (Portsmouth: Wilkes, Breadhower, and Peadle, 1779), pp. 364-365.

The *Stirling Castle* was often called a "haystack" and was widely considered the slowest ship in the fleet.[1] Some may question why the captain who had freed Canada from the clutches of the American colonists was given such a command, but it should instead be viewed as a nod to Douglas' abilities and his reputation as a problem-solver. As proof of this, Douglas managed to get his ship up to snuff and played a prominent part in the First Battle of Ushant, often called the Battle of Brest, as part of Vice-Admiral Sir Robert Harland's division. It was a conflict that the British, by all accounts, should have won. Instead, the French fleet was able to escape, and each side actually accused the other of running from the fight and claimed victory.

After leaving Spithead on 9 July 1778, Admiral Augustus (later Viscount) Keppel was hoping to confront the French fleet. Many of Keppel's men were either new to the service, or were out of practice, not the least of whom was Keppel himself, who had not fought since the Seven Years' War. Keppel had refused to fight the American colonists on political grounds, but now that the French were involved he was called into service. Despite having major differences with Sandwich and the Admiralty, he was given the command of the Channel Fleet since he was the most senior admiral available, and had gained such a good reputation in the former war.

Keppel's fleet of thirty ships of the line came across a French fleet of twenty-nine under Admiral Louis Guillouet, Comte d'Orvilliers, on 23 July. As usual, the French were hoping to avoid a fight, so D'Orvilliers attempted to escape, and the two fleets maneuvered under shifting winds for days. Keppel was finally able to force an action during a heavy rain storm on 27 July, approximately one hundred miles west of the small island of Ushant, off the northwestern coast of France. Most of the British ships were still in good shape following the initial stages of the battle, and Keppel signaled his fleet to turn about and pursue the French, who had gained the windward, but they managed to escape. No ships were sunk or captured on either side.

There were numerous problems with the way Keppel directed the battle, but probably the main reason the French fleet was able

---

[1] *The Georgian Era: Memoirs of the Most Eminent Persons, Who Have Flourished in Great Britain, from the Accession of George the First to the Demise of George the Fourth, in Four Volumes. Volume II* (London: Vizetelly, Branston and Co., 1833), p. 506.

to escape was that the rear division of Admiral Sir Hugh Palliser, his second in command, did not come back around and rejoin the fight as Keppel had signaled. Palliser later claimed his ship, the *Formidable*, was too damaged, but there were some who believed that the admiral, who was a Tory, wanted to see Keppel, a Whig, fail to claim victory for political reasons.

Following the battle and in a politically charged atmosphere, supporters of Admiral Keppel began to criticize Palliser both privately and publicly. Finally, in October, a newspaper published a letter from a naval officer who had participated in the battle (probably Keppel's nephew) that accused Palliser of being responsible for the problems at Ushant. Palliser confronted Keppel and asked him publicly to renounce the accusations, but Keppel refused. This caused Palliser to publish his own account of the battle in several newspapers and publicly demand a court martial for Keppel. Palliser charged that Keppel had gone against the sacrosanct *Fighting Instructions* of the Admiralty by not reforming his line following a general chase to catch the French fleet.

At the trial, the always-loyal Sir Charles Douglas testified on Keppel's behalf, despite being a conservative himself, and said nothing to incriminate the Admiral.[1] The evidence presented by the prosecution was called into question when it was revealed that the logbooks from some of the ships that had participated in the battle had been altered. To the great delight of his supporters, Keppel was exonerated. Palliser was later court-martialed himself, but it only resulted in his censure for not keeping his commander better informed of the condition of his ship during the fight.

One of the more interesting aspects of reading a transcript of the testimony of any historical figure, including Charles Douglas, is the ability to get a real sense of how that person spoke. When compared to most of the other witnesses who testified at the court martial, Douglas comes across as far more educated, refined, and articulate, especially considering he had spent his life at sea from the age of twelve. Most of his answers are much longer than the one or two sentences given by nearly every other witness, of which there were dozens. For example, whereas the previous witness, Captain Kingsmill of the *Vigilant*, answered several questions with "No, it was not," "No, certainly not," or simply, "No," Sir Charles

---

[1] For Douglas' testimony, see *The Trial of the Honouralbe Augustus Keppel, Admiral of the Blue Squadron, at a Court Martial* (Portsmouth: Messrs. J. Wilkes, Breadhower, and Peadle, 1779), pp. 361-365.

answered basically the same questions with answers such as "By no means; to the best of my knowledge, they did endeavor to avoid it," and, "To the best of my knowledge and remembrance it could be no other."[1]

In early 1779, Douglas became captain of a larger ship in the Channel Fleet, known as the *Duke*, with 98 guns. His most prominent role while commanding this ship was in the second Relief of Gibraltar in April of 1781, exactly one year prior to the greatest battle in which he took part. The French and Spanish, whose combined fleets now outnumbered the Royal Navy, attempted to capture Gibraltar from the British in June of 1779, and lay siege for four years, making it one of the longest continuous sieges in history. But there were several successful attempts by the British to break the blockade, starting with the one by Sir George Rodney in February of 1780, in which he was able to bring in supplies and over one thousand reinforcements. The Second Relief of Gibraltar began on 13 March 1781, with twenty-eight ships of the line led by Vice-Admiral George Darby, and five more on their way to India joining them, as well as a convoy of supply ships. The *Duke* was one of the original twenty-eight, and Douglas had on board the Fourteenth Regiment, led by General Urquhart, with whom he became good friends.[2]

The British ships entered the Bay of Gibraltar on 12 April 1781 and were able to anchor there. But the next day, the besiegers opened fire from land and from small gunboats, each with a single 26-pounder. Darby sent the transports in with three ships of the line, and they were able to unload the supplies despite the harassment of the besiegers. In fact, the gunboats did very little real damage to the British ships. The relief was a success. Once again, Douglas had done his part for king and country, and his good fortune in battle continued.

Although Douglas had testified in favor of his commander-in-chief following the Battle of Ushant, it is readily apparent that he was frustrated by the fact that the Royal Navy had been unable to crush the French fleet as it should have. As merely a captain, he could not do much about the system of signals or the leadership

---

[1] *The Trial of the Honorable Augustus Keppel*, pp. 360-364.

[2] "General Urquhart." *Public Characters of 1803-1804* (London: Richard Philips, 1804), p. 501.

abilities of his superiors and peers, but one area where he felt he could contribute was in the improvement of naval gunnery in the British fleet of the time. His service at the Home Station in the years between Quebec and the Saints is, therefore, not known for his taking part in the First Battle of Ushant or the Second Relief of Gibraltar, but rather for the naval gunnery innovations he instituted on his ship during this time.

CHAPTER SIX

NAVAL GUNNERY
INNOVATIONS

Both these last improvements were initiated by Sir Charles Douglas, one of Collingwood's few equals in the art [of naval gunnery].[1]

After Spanish Admiral Don Frederico Gravina toured British ships as he visited the dockyard at Portsmouth in 1793, he decided that the main reasons for the superiority of British gunnery were better gun carriages, the use of flintlocks for firing, and the constant drilling of gun crews.[2] The man responsible for the improved carriages and the widespread use of flintlocks, as well as other improvements, was Sir Charles Douglas, who had died four years earlier. He was also known for championing the drilling of naval gunners, something that began to lapse a short time later until his son, Sir Howard, convinced the Royal Navy of its necessity.

In ancient times, naval warfare consisted of boarding parties, ships ramming one another, and archers firing at one another from the decks. Once gunpowder was introduced, large guns, or cannons, were used to discharge all manner of shot, including stone, at opposing crews. By the time of Henry VIII in the 16th Century, both iron and bronze guns were being used to turn ships

---

[1] Max Adams, *Trafalgar's Lost Hero: Admiral Lord Collingwood and the Defeat of Napoleon* (Hoboken, NJ: Wiley, 2005), p. 119.

[2] Dr. Nicholas Tracy, "Naval Tactics in the Age of Sail," *The Trafalgar Companion* (Oxford: Osprey Publishing, 2005), p. 126.

into floating batteries. The objective became damaging an enemy ships' hull and rigging, as well as its crew. But improvements to the technology were slow in coming, and by the end of the 18th Century not much had changed. The fact is naval gunnery advanced little between the time of Henry VIII and George III, so any innovations were very welcome.

In the 1750s, the Admiralty had ordered that the type of locks used on muskets be installed on the guns of naval vessels, but this was not accomplished to any great extent, and by the time of the War of American Independence, the method appears to have completely fallen from use. Brian Tunstall suggests that, after Admiral Hawke objected to the locks because it increased the danger of the tin priming tubes flying out and injuring gun crews, the entire plan may even have been dropped.[1]

Douglas wanted all the guns on his new ship in the Channel Fleet, the *Duke*, 98 guns, to be outfitted with them, but the Admiralty refused. So he used his own money to purchase enough musket locks for all of his guns, and used wire to attach them.

The Barham Papers contain so many letters from Douglas to Charles Middleton, Lord Barham, at the Admiralty, filled with technical information on improvements, that the editor began to excise portions and simply state that Douglas described things in "tedious detail."[2] The letters seem to indicate that Douglas had almost an obsession regarding making improvements to the *Duke*, especially where the guns were concerned. One letter, on 5 May 1779, contained plans for a ship's keel fixed on hinges, which he believed would make a ship stiffer and make less leeway. The editor notes, "The description is very long, and is here given in short abstract."[3]

A second letter, dated 12 July 1779, suggested adding Carronades to the poop deck of his ship. These short, powerful "smashers" proved very destructive at close range, and eventually became standard on ships of the Royal Navy. Nathan Miller credits Douglas with the addition of carronades to Rodney's fleet later on (as did the author George Cupples), which was probably one of the

---

[1] Brian Tunstall and Nicholas Tracy (editor), *Naval Warfare in the Age of Sail* (Edison, NJ: Wellfleet Press, 1990), p. 182.

[2] Laughton. P.274.

[3] *Ibid.*, p. 267.

main factors in the victory at the Saints.[1] However, Peter Trew specifically states that carronades were not one of the changes to be attributed to Douglas.[2] Regardless, his letter requesting their installation early on (the Carron factory had only applied to the Admiralty for their approval about a year earlier) shows that Douglas understood their effectiveness and favored their use.

Douglas also wanted to add three twenty-four pounders to each side of the quarter-deck, "where rigging is not in the way." He went on to describe how he had figured out a way to allow the guns to swivel easier and wider:

> By the means, then, of bolts placed in the side, right in the middle between every two guns, into which we occasionally hook their tackles, we are able to point all of them, without using a crow or handspike, where knees called standards do not interfere, full four points before or abaft the beam, which I presume is to a degree of obliquity until now unknown in the navy.[3]

This was an understatement. Up until then, guns basically pointed straight ahead at right angles to the ship's head, and had to be fired when the target was passing by. Douglas' rigging allowed guns to swivel ninety degrees (forty-five degrees to each side), which made a huge difference not only in aiming the guns, but in the gun crews' ability to fire at targets that were approaching or moving away. The Naval Institute's *Sea Power* describes the enhancement in this way:

> The old rule had been "two or three quick broadsides in passing," but now the special tackle enabled British gun crews to train their guns up to four points ahead or astern of the beam. The result was that the British ship would fire two or tree broadsides both before and after the guns of a French ship could be brought to bear, and, while they were opposite, the British were able to fire a great deal more rapidly.[4]

---

[1] Nathan Miller, *Broadsides: The Age of Fighting Sail, 1775-1815* (New York: Jon Wiley & Sons, 2000), p. 89; Cupples, p. 138.

[2] Peter Trew, *Rodney and the Breaking of the* Line (South Yorkshire, England: Pen & Sword, 2006), p. 147.

[3] Laughton, p. 268.

[4] E.B. Potter (ed.), *Sea Power* (Annapolis: Naval Institute Press, 1981), p. 49.

In September of that year, Douglas wrote with news of more improvements. After complaining of having continuing problems with the stiffness of the *Duke* and having to take on additional salt water as a result, he described his solution to not having enough room to fully discharge the cannons:

> A wedge properly adapted is placed behind each truck, to make up for the reduction of space to recoil in, in firing to windward or in rolling weather. The gun first ascends the wedges by rotation, and when stopped by the cleats which cross the back parts thereof, performs the remainder of her recoil as a sledge so feebly as scarce to bring her breeching tight. In thus firing lee guns with a steady breeze and without rolling to windward, if any wedges are at all necessary two are sufficient. The bottoms thereof, to augment their friction against the deck, are pinked, tarred, and rubbed with very rough sand or with coarse coal dust.[1]

After continuing on in the letter to tell his friend of the death of his wife and son, he added a postscript about his order to have another port cut abaft on the quarter-deck of his ship so that he may add one more gun to the broadside, "nor can it weaken her in any degree as to shorten her duration a single hour. My carpenter is of the same opinion."[2]

A couple of years later, in September of 1781, Douglas wrote to Barham again about changes he had made to the guns on the *Duke*. He had been worried about the breechings breaking (which had happened on other ships) due to the shortened distance for recoiling because of his earlier changes. The danger of breechings (ropes that secured the gun) breaking was immense, as the cannon could then move around the deck, injuring crewmembers and, potentially, even going through the side of the ship. Therefore, "it became not only expedient, but even necessary to apply some gradual, self-managing check to their recoiling, for the preservation of their breeching." His solution was to use springs made of tempered steel, which worked so well that he said the breechings were "infallibly secured against breaking."[3] He added that a gun's recoil could be checked even better if two shot, slung together, were hung in the middle of the spring. This also resulted in the

---

[1] Laughton, pp. 269-70.

[2] *Ibid.*, p 171.

[3] *Id.*

wedges fixed on the carriage sides to have an inclining plane, which was another advantageous modification.

He explained a model gun he was sending to the Admiralty, which had such springs and wedges, and a new type of muzzle he had designed. The new muzzle was "of great consequence, by saving a motion in oblique spring, and by extending its latitude of pointing in all the four different senses of pointing guns." [1] He even added protuberances on each side of the touchholes of the model gun to hinder the grains of powder from falling to the deck while priming—something that had been a fire hazard in the past due to sparks.

Douglas also sent along samples of some perforated goose quills pre-filled with powder, which he had been using instead of the standard tin priming tubes, and flannel cartridges. The quills were "safer, tidier and more certain than loose powder from a powder horn." [2] They were also better than those made of tin because they did not corrode, and sometimes the tin primers were known to fly out and wound gun crews. [3] The flannel cartridges were much more efficient than the paper ones in current use, especially since some paper would remain and have to be wormed out of the gun after every shot.

A letter of the following November described an apparatus that Douglas had invented for checking the severe recoil of guns during a storm, when the deck is slick and the ship is rolling more than usual. The complicated series of rope, bolts, and grommets also helped with running the gun out.

After Douglas became Rodney's captain-of-the-fleet, the same alterations made to the *Duke* were made to at least two other ships of the fleet, the flagship *Formidable* (which had been Palliser's ship at Ushant) and the *Arrogant*. In Douglas' letter to Barham of 28 April 1782, he was able to brag about the efficacy of his improvements, having literally tested them under fire during the Battle of the Saints on 12 April:

> Such ships as have their guns fitted accordingly, derived unspeakable advantage from some improvements lately made in the use of naval artillery, their fire having been so very quick and so very well directed, and extending so far

---

[1] *Ibid.*, pp. 272-273.

[2] John Munday, *Naval Cannon*, Aylesbury (UK: Shire Publications Ltd, 1987), p. 13.

[3] Robison, p. 369.

to the right and left, that the French cannot comprehend how they came to lose so many men, and we so few, on the late bloody day; for they were generally so mauled by the ships alluded to as to be most part driven from their quarters before they could bring their guns to bear upon us. The fire of our centre, consisting of three three-deckers, was astonishing indeed.[1]

In other words, Douglas' suggestions had worked beautifully. He added that not a single one of his goose-quill tubes failed, and none of the guns on the *Formidable* or the *Duke* required worming as long as the flannel cartridges lasted. None of the locks he had installed on the *Duke* failed either, and only one out of 126 even needed a new flint throughout the entire battle.

Though about eighty men short at quarters, the Duke, from the improvements alluded to, fired sometimes fully from both sides, and even with as much ease as if they had been exercising; nor did a single atom of gunpowder catch fire by accident on board of her, she having, as usual, and as now is becoming the practice, as well as the Formidable and divers other ships, used wetted wads.[2]

The last line regarding wetted wads referenced another change Douglas had made for the safety of the gunners.

Douglas could not resist writing a follow-up letter on 4 May regarding the battle, to say how even he was surprised by how well the wider range of firing had worked for those ships that had been outfitted with the ability to do so. Captain Gardner of the *Duke* told Rodney that he was able to fire twice as many shot as he would have before the improvements. Also, when the *Ville de Paris* edged down upon the *Arrogant*, de Grasse, thinking he was out of its line of fire, was surprised to find his enemy able to fire a broadside attack. Lieutenant Butler of the *Formidable* claimed that they were able to fire two, and sometimes three, times to every one shot from the French guns.[3]

Ironically, the last letter from Sir Charles Douglas published in the *Barham Papers* was written just after the war ended in 1783, and Douglas believed it would no longer be necessary for them to push for his innovations to be taken up by the Admiralty. He suggested to Lord Barham that they should merely hold onto a model

---

[1] Laughton, pp. 280-81.

[2] *Ibid.*, p. 282.

[3] *Ibid.*, p. 284.

or two, and that the improvements should "dwindle into seeming disregard and oblivion."[1] In this he could not have been more wrong, with the Napoleonic Wars and other political unrest just around the corner.

After the success at the Battle of the Saints, the entire British fleet eventually made most of the changes Douglas had implemented, although there was some resistance from certain captains, so the changes were not immediate. It was not until Sir Charles' son, Sir Howard Douglas, came into prominence as a military scientist and author that such drastic changes would be made again.

---

[1] *Ibid.*, p. 287.

CHAPTER SEVEN

THE BATTLE OF
THE SAINTS

We had a great deal to do, Sir, and I believe you will allow
we did a great deal.

Sir Charles Douglas' modest response
when questioned publicly regarding
the breaking of the line maneuver [1]

It was the early morning hours of 12 April 1782, and Sir George
Brydges Rodney, Admiral of the White, was spoiling for a fight.
The French fleet under the comte de Grasse was on its way to meet
a small Spanish fleet so that they could together invade Jamaica,
one of the few Caribbean islands still held by the British. If Rodney, now British Commander-in-Chief of the West Indies, could
catch Admiral de Grasse in time, he might just prevent this from
happening. He came upon the French in the channel between Dominica and a small group of islands known as the Isles de Saintes,
and both fleets drew up their battle lines. What happened next
would change the course of history, and incite one of the great
controversies of the period. An unusual maneuver by the British
ships, rarely attempted in a battle up to that time, led to a decima-
tion of the French fleet from which it never recovered. The credit

---

[1] David Hannay, *English Men of Action: Rodney* (London: McMillan and
Co., 1891),p. 210.

for the maneuver, however, would later be fought among members of the same side.

By the end of the eighteenth century, naval tactics had become stale. Admirals and captains were required to follow the rules of battle imposed on them from above. Known as the "Sailing and Fighting Instructions," these directives had come about after a great deal of trial-and-error at the beginning of the Age of Sail, when the limits of fighting in vessels dependent upon the wind and other weather conditions began to be understood. Following these instructions, as well as common sense, a style of fighting had come about where two fleets would line up, one ship behind the other, then pass one another going in the same or opposite directions, shooting their cannons as each ship went by. Ships large enough to form up in such a battle line became known as "ships of the line," "battle-line ships," or simply "battleships." This would continue until one side surrendered or escaped. Naval battles of the time became quite orderly, and this prevented ships on the same side from causing damage to one another either from their guns or due to collisions. It also meant that the side with the greater firepower generally won, and that the winning side was often nearly as damaged as the loser. But it also led to a great many stalemates, especially since the French tended to attempt to escape the more powerful British ships, including firing into their rigging to slow them down.

This is not to say that officers of the Royal Navy never deviated from the Fighting Instructions. In 1744, Admiral Sir Thomas Mathews fought against a combined Franco-Spanish fleet at the Battle of Toulan and went against the Instructions. His maneuver, which may even have been an attempt to break the enemy line, met with such failure that he was court-martialed, along with his second in command.[1] This and other examples led naval commanders to be highly reticent about varying their tactics. At least that way, if they failed, they could still claim they were simply following orders. The Battle of the Saints (known to the French as the Battle of Dominica) changed all of that.

Sir Charles Douglas became Rodney's captain-of-the-fleet, replacing Walter Young, on 24 November 1781. According to the famous *Biographia Navalis* by John Charnock, this gave Douglas the temporary rank of rear-admiral, but in reality he was the highest ranking captain and, as chief of staff to the admiral, received the pay and wore the uniform of a rear-admiral. All orders from a

---

[1] Trew, p. 15.

captain-of-the-fleet were considered to be coming from the admiral himself, and had to be obeyed, even by other flag officers who outranked him. Some sources refer to Douglas as Rodney's "flag captain," although this is not entirely accurate, since the flag captain was actually the captain of the admiral's flag ship (usually a junior captain), who oversaw the day-to-day operations of the ship. The captain-of-the-fleet was also referred to as the "first captain," with the flag captain being the "second captain." Rodney's flag captain was John Symons (sometimes spelled Symonds or Simmons). To complicate matters, James, Lord Cranstoun, also came on board the *Formidable* just prior to the battle as a supernumerary captain, and acted as a prize captain following the battle. As a result, some sources mistakenly state that Cranstoun acted as captain of the *Formidable* during the battle.

Rodney left London on 2 December, and Portsmouth in early January 1782 after being told by Sandwich that the fate of the Empire was in his hands. The only islands in the West Indies still under British control were Jamaica, Barbados, St. Lucia, and Antigua. Admiral de Grasse's plan was to rendezvous with twelve Spanish ships of the line at St. Domingo, along with fifteen thousand Spanish Troops under General Don Galvez, then commence the invasion of Jamaica, the largest and richest of Britain's remaining Caribbean holdings.

On 9 April, the British van under Admiral Sir Samuel Hood closed on the French fleet, but the center and rear divisions were unable to follow due to a lack of wind. As a result, Hood's division received a great deal of damage from de Grasse's forces and the French were able to escape. Rodney ordered the damaged division to the rear, and Rear-Admiral Sir Francis Samuel Drake's forward, and the next morning the pursuit continued.

De Grasse, who had no interest in fighting the British fleet, had sent one of his ships, the *Zelé* (74 guns), in to Guadeloupe for repairs after it was involved in at least three collisions in the past few days, including one with his own flagship, the *Ville de Paris*, the largest vessel afloat at that time. Around five a.m. on the 12th, the British spotted the *Zelé* being towed and Hood sent four ships after it. De Grasse decided to protect the damaged ship from her pursuers and changed course, and by six a.m., with no chance of outrunning Rodney, formed a line of battle on a southerly course.

Rodney answered by forming his line in a north-northwesterly direction in an attempt to get to windward of the French. A short time later, Douglas went to the Admiral's cabin where he was resting, and informed Rodney that "Providence has given you your enemy broad on the lee bow."[1] Rodney ordered his ships within one cable of the French. At this point Rodney had thirty-six ships and de Grasse was down to thirty, having lost three in the previous few days, although the French still had more total firepower, calculated by Douglas to be 4396 more pounds of metal.

De Grasse attempted to stay as far away as possible to minimize the damage the British might inflict and to attempt an escape as soon as possible, and several of the ships in his van were able to skirt the British line. But shortly after seven-thirty a.m., the *Marlborough* (74), the lead British ship, closed on the French line and began to engage the *Brave* (74), which was the ninth ship in line, since they were also in reverse order.

As a result of British superiority in gunnery, including carronades and the improvements Douglas had made to some of the ships, the French soon began to take heavy damage. De Grasse signaled his ships twice to turn back in the opposite direction when he realized there would be no wind as his line moved toward Dominica, but his captains were unable to comply because the British had moved within pistol shot of them. Then a change in the direction of the wind caused further confusion in the French line and opened up spaces between their ships. Suddenly there was a gap between the *Glorieux*, the ship directly opposite the *Formidable*, and the *Diademe* following it.

An eyewitness account of the event was written by Charles Dashwood, a seventeen-year-old (although most sources mistakenly say thirteen) *aide-de-camp* to Rodney and Douglas at the time.[2] Dashwood, who later became a vice-admiral and a knight himself, gave a detailed description of the exchange between Rodney and Douglas. According to Dashwood's letter to Sir Howard Douglas, Sir Charles was leaning on the hammocks and staring out at the French line, when he suddenly exclaimed, "Dash! Where's Sir George?" When Dashwood replied he was in the aft cabin, Sir Charles headed in that direction and met with Rodney, who was coming from the cabin and was close to the wheel. Then Sir Charles bowed and said:

> "Sir George, I give you the joy of victory!" "Poh!" said the chief, as if half angry, "the day is not half won yet." "Break

---

[1] Miller, *Broadsides*, p. 92.

[2] Sylvanus Urban, "Sir Charles Dashwood," *The Gentleman's Magazine*, Vol. 28, July to December 1847. (London : John Bowyer Nichols and Son), Obituary, p. 636.

the line, Sir George!" said your [Sir Howard's] father, "the day is your own, and I will insure you the victory." "No," said the admiral, "I will not break my line." After another request and another refusal, Sir Charles desired the helm to be put a-port; Sir Charles ordered it to starboard. On your father ordering it again to port, the admiral sternly said, "Remember, Sir Charles, that I am commander-in-chief—starboard, sir," addressing the master, who, during this controversy, had placed the helm amidships. Both the admiral and the captain then separated; the former going aft, the latter forward. In the course of a couple of minutes or so, each turned and again met nearly on the same spot." Then Sir Charles quietly and coolly again addressed the chief—"Only break the line, Sir George, and the day is your own." The admiral then said, in a quick and hurried way, "Well, well, do as you like;" and immediately turned around and walked into the aft cabin. The words "Port the helm!" were scarcely uttered, when Sir Charles ordered me down with directions to commence firing on the larboard side. On my return to the quarter deck, I found the *Formidable* passing between two French ships, each nearly touching us. We were followed by the *Namur*, and the rest of the ships astern; and from that moment the victory was decided in our favor.[1]

Rodney's flagship, the *Formidable*, had sailed toward and through the French line (thus "breaking the line") and several other British ships in Rodney's division followed suit: the *Namur*, the *St. Albans*, the *Canada*, the *Repulse*, and the *Ajax*. Furthermore, the *Duke*, commanded by Captain Alan Gardner, which was ahead of the flagship, broke the French line as well, probably because he had no other option, but perhaps because he saw what was happening behind him in the line. Toward the back of the British line of battle, Commodore Edmund Affleck followed the signal from Rodney's flagship to tack, and took the *Bedford*

---

[1] This account can be found in many places, but was first widely published in the article "Rodney's Battle of 12th April, 1782: A Statement of Some Important Facts, Supported by Authentic Documents, Relating to the Operation of Breaking the Enemy's Line, as Practiced for the First Time in the Celebrated Battle of 12th April, 1782," *Quarterly Review*, vol. XLII, no. LXXXIII, January & March, 1830 (London: John Murray, 1830), p. 64. No author was credited, but it is understood to have been written by Sir John Barrow, Lord of the Admiralty.

through the line, followed by all of the rear division commanded by Vice-Admiral Sir Samuel (later Lord) Hood.[1]

Because nearly all of the guns on the ships were located on the sides, the British ships were able to fire away at the hapless French vessels, which were practically unable to return fire. The ships were also extremely close together, in some cases within pistol shot, which was always an advantage for the British and their more powerful guns and carronades. The French fleet was devastated, and many ships were disabled or captured, including de Grasse's flagship, the *Ville de Paris*. Sir Gilbert Blane, Physician to the Fleet, later said in a letter that he and Douglas embraced when they saw the French flag hauled down, "stupefied as it were by an ecstasy of joy."[2] De Grasse himself was taken prisoner after having fought until his crew was unable to continue firing. In fact, he was one of the only ones left standing amid the carnage aboard his flagship, and was slightly wounded himself. He surrendered his sword to Lord Cranstoun, the prize captain, and was brought aboard the *Formidable* the next morning. Sir Charles Douglas, who had met de Grasse in 1747 as a midshipman on the *Centurion* when de Grasse had been captured as an ensign aboard the *Gloire*, introduced him to Dr. Blane and Captain William Cornwallis. According to W.H. Adams, Douglas said in French, "This is the physician of our fleet, who is almost skillful enough to resuscitate the dead"; to which the Comte responded, "And perhaps to put to death the living."[3] De Grasse was quick to blame his captains for the defeat, and was able to recover quickly from the trauma of the battle, to the point of actually enjoying himself fishing for sharks with the British soon afterward. De Grasse would later be transported to England, where his sword was returned to him by King George III himself, and he was allowed to return to France.

---

[1] Some authors point out that Affleck should get as much credit as Rodney or Douglas for breaking the line, since he did the same. However, in *Naval Evolutions,* Sir Howard Douglas used the logs of Affleck's own ship, the *Bedford,* to prove that the commodore was following his admiral's signals and not acting on his own initiative. As for Gardner, most analysts believe he had not choice but to break through the line in order to prevent a collision with the confused French ships.

[2] Stephen Brown, *Scurvy: How a Surgeon, a Mariner, and Gentleman Solved the Greatest Medical Mystery of the Age of Sail* (New York: Thomas Dunne Books, 2003), p. 172.

[3] W.H. Adams, *Eminent Sailors* (London: George Routledge and Sons, 1882), p. 156.

Vice-Admiral Hood, Rodney's second in command, gave chase after the rest of the French fleet along with several other ships, but Rodney called him back. Hood, never one to turn down a chance at criticizing another officer, wrote scathing letters to the admiralty to let them know about his objections to this move, and stating his belief that twenty more French ships could have been captured, ostensibly taking France out of the war altogether. [1]

Probably unbeknownst to Hood, Sir Charles Douglas completely agreed. Although Hood was very vocal in his contempt for Douglas, it is unknown whether the feeling was mutual, since Douglas' character and loyalty would never have allowed him to criticize a superior officer. [2] But one thing is certain: Douglas gave Rodney the same advice Hood did about chasing the fleet, and, as A. T. Mahan said, "...the chief-of-staff was so much mortified by the failure, and by the manner in which the admiral received his suggestions, as seriously to contemplate resigning his position." [3] True to form, Douglas later defended Rodney's decision to Hood and kept his own objections to himself, perhaps magnifying Hood's dislike for him. [4] Rodney did allow Hood to go after the French with ten ships of the line five days later, and Hood managed to capture two more ships in the Strait of Mona on 19 April.

Rodney, who was not usually in the habit of complimenting others, had this to say about Douglas in his official dispatch following the battle: "My own captain, Sir Charles Douglas, merits

---

[1] Hood's letters to this effect can be found in David Hannay (ed.), *Letters Written by Sir Samuel Hood (Viscount Hood) in 1781-2-3, Vol. II.* (London: Publications of the Naval Records Society, 1895. Elibron Classics reprint, 2007), pp. 101-108; and Sir John Knox Laughton (ed.), *Letters and Papers of Charles, Lord Barham, Admiral of the Red Squadron, 1758-1813,* (London: Navy Records Society, 1907. Elibron Classics edition, 2007), pp.176-179.

[2] Sir John Laughton, the editor of Lord Barham's papers, believed Hood's feelings toward Douglas were exacerbated by Hood's liver problems at the time. Laughton, p. 179 (footnote).

[3] Alfred T. Mahan, *The Influence of Sea Power Upon History, 1660-1783.* (New York: Barnes & Noble Books, 2004. First published in 1890.), p. 496.

[4] Hannay, *Hood,* p. 105. For more on Douglas' refusal to acknowledge his agreement with Hood out of loyalty to Rodney, see A.T. Mahan, *Types of Naval Officers Drawn from the History of the British Navy* (Boston: Little, Brown, and Company, 1901), pp. 247-248.

every thing I can possibly say. His unremitted diligence and activity greatly eased me in the unavoidable fatigue of the day."[1]

Regardless of the details that would later be debated, it was considered a tremendous victory by most, with several important consequences: First, it ruined France's plan to invade Jamaica, which remained a British colony. Second, it reasserted Britain's dominance at sea after huge losses during the Revolutionary War, allowing Britain to save face at the treaty negotiations a short time later. Third and finally, it changed naval warfare for as long as battles continued to be fought between sailing ships (well into the nineteenth century), including the all-important Battle of Trafalgar, where Admiral Horatio Nelson defeated Napoleon's fleet using similar tactics. It is even said that Nelson specifically went into that battle with the intention of copying Rodney.

Furthermore, the complete imbalance in casualties shows the great extent to which the British dominated the battle. British casualties were reported to be only 243 dead and 816 wounded. While there are no official numbers for the French, more than 5,000 were captured and it is estimated that as many as 3,000 may have been killed (six of whom were captains). This number was magnified due to the large number of soldiers that were being transported to Jamaica. In fact, just on de Grasse's flagship alone, there were 400 killed and 700 wounded, more total casualties than in the entire British fleet.

Before the Battle of the Saints, the British government had been so unhappy with Rodney's recent performance in the West Indies that (unbeknownst to Rodney) his replacement, Admiral Pigot, had already been sent to relieve him. Following the battle, amidst celebrations all over the country, the government was forced to acknowledge the great victory.[2] Rodney was made a

---

[1] Godfrey Basil Mundy, *The Life and Correspondence of the Late Admiral Lord Rodney, Vol. II* (London: John Murray, 1830. Elibron Classics reprint, 2007.), p. 257.

[2] Stephen Conway, "'A Joy Unknown for Years Past': The American War Britishness and the Celebration of Rodney's Victory at the Saints," *History*, April 2001, Vol. 86, Issue 282 (London: Accessed online through Proquest at <http://search.ebscohost.com.ezproxy.apus.edu/login.aspx?direct=true&db=aph&AN=4511560&site=ehost-live>.)

baron, and parliament officially thanked him for his service.[1] Hood was made a peer of Ireland as well, Rear-Admiral Drake a baronet, and Commodore Affleck both an admiral and a baronet.

Unfortunately for Douglas, he received neither honorary nor monetary remuneration for his part in the battle, despite an attempt by Lord Sandwich to convince the House of Lords to correct the injustice. The reasons why the captain of the fleet did not share in the awards of the day can only be speculated upon, as they were by *The Gentleman's Magazine* in 1791, where it was assumed that it was simply a matter of Douglas already being a baronet, and therefore he would have to have been elevated to the peerage, putting him on equal standing with Rodney and Hood and above his senior officers, Drake and Affleck. It was, therefore, assumed that Douglas was actually a victim of his own earlier success.

Furthermore, the credit for the breaking of the line maneuver was to become a great controversy fought in books and periodicals over the course of the first half of the eighteenth century. Though the exact truth will probably never be determined, a thorough examination of the evidence available strongly favors one side: that of Sir Charles Douglas.

---

[1] Kenneth Breen, "George Bridges, Lord Rodney." *Precursors of Nelson: British Admirals of the Eighteenth Century*, Richard Harding and Peter LeFevre (eds.), (Mechanicsburg, PA: Stockpole Books, 2000), p. 245.

CHAPTER EIGHT
POST-REVOLUTION YEARS AND DEATH

He was a very good, a very brave, and a very honest man. [1]

The Naval Chronicle

Shortly after the Battle of the Saints, Admiral Pigot arrived to take Rodney's place, and Douglas remained Pigot's captain-of-the-fleet for the remainder of the war, traveling to New York and Jamaica. Following the Treaty of Paris, Douglas returned to England, arriving in July of 1783. He was once again made a commodore [2] and was appointed as commander-in-chief of the North American station at Halifax in October of that year. Douglas had no wish to make the journey in winter, and W. J. Stairs describes in a family history how his grandfather befriended Douglas and journeyed with him and Lady Douglas throughout many islands in the West Indies before arriving in Nova Scotia on 29 May 1784. [3] After attempting to reach Halifax in winter, Douglas' flagship, the *Assis-*

---

[1] *The Naval Chronicle for 1805: Containing a General and Biographical History of the Royal Navy of the United Kingdom; with a Variety of Original Papers of Nautical Subjects* (London: I. Gold, 1805), p. 445. See also Hadden, p. 300 (footnote).

[2] At that time, commodore was a temporary rank given to senior captains in charge of squadrons or small fleets.

[3] W.J. Stairs and Susan Morrow Stairs, *Family History: Stairs, Morrow, Including Letters, Diaries, Essays, Poems, etc.* (Halifax, Nova Scotia: McAlpine Publishing Company, Ltd., 1906), p. 223.

tance, was forced by inclement weather to land at Sandy Hook, New Jersey, where three men attempted to desert during a blizzard. Fourteen crew members were sent to search for the deserters and were all killed in the storm, including marine Lieutenant Hamilton Douglas Halyburton. Halyburton was the son of Sholto Douglas, 15th Earl of Morton, which made him a relative of Sir Charles.

Because of the harsh conditions, Douglas gave up trying to make it to Nova Scotia during the winter and instead sailed for Barbados, and also stopped at Dominica, Antigua, Monserrat, St. Christopher, and Nevis on the journey. The people of the West Indies reportedly treated him as a hero for his role in the Battle of the Saints, although he was always quick to downplay his part. Before arriving in Halifax, Douglas also stopped at the newly-built Loyalist settlement of Shelburne in Nova Scotia.

While commander-in-chief of North America, Sir Charles was adamant about enforcing the Treaty of Paris to the letter, to the point of driving away Americans who came ashore to cut wood for fires in order to melt the blubber from the whales they had killed in the Gulf of St. Lawrence. Another of his duties there entailed protecting British coal mines from foreigners as well as local residents. In July 1784, just a couple of months after his arrival, Douglas ordered HMS *Resource* to Spanish River to stop the illegal taking of coal from the area. He also dispatched HMS *Hermione* to St. Pierre and Miquelon upon reports of the locals digging up coal, and military commanders were ordered to ensure that only those with special permission were allowed to remove coal.

Douglas did not enjoy his time at Halifax, and requested to be recalled less than a year later.[1] It is generally reported that he requested the recall because he came into so much conflict with Henry Duncan, the dockyard commissioner, and Duncan's naval storekeeper, George Thomas, while there. The problem was that Thomas had requested leave prior to Douglas' arrival and had appointed his own temporary replacement, a clerk named John Lawson. Although the storekeeper had been granted permission by the Commissioner, Duncan had left for an inspection and Douglas appointed his own replacement instead, and insisted that Thomas complete a survey of the all the naval stores before taking his

---

[1] Julian Gwyn, *Frigates and Foremasts: the North American Squadron in Nova Scotia Waters, 1745-1815* (Vancouver: UBC Press, 2003), p. 84. Accessed through the APUS Online Research Library.

leave. Thomas ignored Douglas' orders and departed, leaving Lawson in charge of the stores. Douglas subsequently suspended not only Thomas, but also Lawson and the second clerk, Alexander Anderson, for not cooperating with the survey. When Commissioner Duncan returned, he was unhappy with the changes made by Douglas, but cooperated with Douglas' appointee, Frederick Edgecomb, until the Admiralty was consulted. Meanwhile, Douglas had appointed chaplains aboard several of the ships of his squadron, *Ariadne, Resource, and Hermione*, an action with which the Admiralty took issue even though Douglas was confident that it was completely within his power to do so. Whether because of the matter with the storekeeper, the chaplains, or both, Douglas was chastised by the Admiralty for overstepping his bounds, and requested to be recalled, citing "cogent reasons."[1] His request was granted, and he was back in England by late August, 1785, with Commodore Sawyer becoming his replacement in Halifax.

Upon his return to England, Douglas was sent on a mission to Holland, with whom the British government was having problems. The details of his trip were a secret, but it is known that Douglas succeeded in whatever it was he set out to do, as this is given as the explanation as to why King George III insisted on making him a rear-admiral above so many other senior captains. Whatever the covert business was that he conducted on behalf of the Crown, it prevented him from hoisting his flag.

A glimpse into Douglas' private life at this time is available through a letter he wrote to his friend and relative, Adam Smith, in 1786. The letter survives not because of Sir Charles, but because it is part of the collection of Smith's papers in the Glasgow University Library. Douglas discussed his sister Helena's legal troubles over her lawsuit for defamation brought on by a neighbor, and asked Smith to visit her and try to make her feel better. The case had been going on for a few years already as a result of Helena accusing Elizabeth Chalmers, wife of Archibald Scott, of having multiple affairs, and Helena had refused to attend any social functions to which Mrs. Scott had been invited. She even went as far as to say that none of her neighbor's children were her husband's. The case eventually went on for ten years, with Helena's attorney changing defenses from denying that she had started the rumors

---

[1] Gwyn, Julian. *Ashore and Afloat: The British Navy and the Halifax Naval Yard Before 1820* (Ottawa: University of Ottawa Press, 2004), pp. 84-85

to attempting to prove the accusations were true. But only one witness would testify on Douglas' sister's behalf, and she was eventually found guilty in 1793, and forced to pay £100 in damages, a £10 fine, and £800 in expenses.[1]

Douglas was so worried about his sister's state of mind at that time that he was afraid to tell her in a letter that he was going to be taking his second-oldest son, Charles, away to attend the Royal Naval Academy at Portsmouth. Instead, he also asked Smith to discuss the matter with Helena in person so he could comfort her if she reacted badly. However, in a letter a few years later, it appears that the younger Charles did not go to the Academy at that time, since his education was still an issue.

Douglas was promoted to rear-admiral on 24 September 1787, as noted earlier, above dozens of captains with more seniority. In May and June, 1788, he made a journey back to Holland along with Lieutenant Colonel Moncrief and an engineer named John Finlay to help in obtaining information for the Master General of the Ordnance about the state of defense in the maritime towns of the United Provinces. Douglas had made the arrangements for the trip due to his extensive connections in the Netherlands, and was requested to accompany them and give them whatever assistance they needed.[2] Also in 1788, Catherine the Great included Douglas on a list of British officers she wanted to lure to the Russian Navy after Admiral Samuel Greig's death that same year.

Douglas was again appointed as commander-in-chief of the Halifax station in January 1789, at the express request of none other than King George III himself, once his replacement, Commodore Sawyer, had fulfilled his term. But Sir Charles was never able to take up that command, since on a trip to Edinburgh to visit his family he died of apoplexy on 10 March. Some versions of his death claim he collapsed while entering a public building, but his son's biographer says he died in bed after being ill with a severe headache for most of that day. According to that dramatic account, Sir Charles refused to allow his son, Howard, to close the curtains

---

[1] Leah Leneman. "Defamation in Scotland, 1750-1800," *Continuity and Change*, Number 15 (2). (United Kingdom: Cambridge University Press, 2000), p 214.

[2] A.J.B. Wallace, "A British Officer in Active Service, 1799," *The Annual of the British School at Athens*, Vol. 23, (British School at Athens, 1918/1919), pp. 128 (footnote).

on the windows in the room in which he was lying in bed because everyone was celebrating the recuperation of King George III from a long illness. Howard visited him in his room before going to a dance that was being held as part of the celebration, and Charles died a short time later.

Still another version of Sir Charles' death appeared in *The Gentleman's and London Magazine: or Monthly Chronologer for 1791*. According to this account, Douglas actually attended a ball (probably the same one referred to in Fullom's story) to see his youngest daughter dance for the first time. Around nine p.m., he told his sister he was going to go home to rest due to a severe headache. When she arrived sometime later, he was unconscious on his bed and, unable to wake him, Helena sent for a doctor. However, he remained "insensible" and died the next day at approximately noon.

At the time, his stroke was believed to have been the result of his journey to Scotland, which had been in a mail carriage. Apparently the ride was so jarring that it was thought to have caused blood vessels in his head to burst—an occurrence that his friend, Dr. Knox, had warned him about beforehand. Douglas, having spent his life fighting naval battles, laughed at the thought of being killed by a carriage ride and ignored the doctor's advice.[1]

Shortly before his death, Sir Charles had written a letter, dated 19 February, 1789, to Helena about his pending visit to Scotland. He claimed that his wife, "Lady Douglas," would not be accompanying him because she had caught a cold. This could very well be true, but based on what little is known about the family dynamics at the time, it is also likely that she simply had no desire to go with him. Douglas also mentioned that they would need to discuss the education of his "two boys," Charles and Howard, with one of the options being the Royal Academy at Woolwich and another accompanying Sir Charles to Canada. Either way, a primary concern of his was that they learn French and Dutch, two of the languages in which he was fluent himself. The letter ended with the statement, "Nobody is to make mention to me anything of my undutiful eldest daughter!" This unusual behavior was prompted by Lydia's aforementioned marriage to Reverend Richard Bingham, of whom Sir Charles did not approve. Douglas added a codicil to his will in November of 1788 stating that if she married Richard Bingham,

---

[1] "Memoirs of Sir Charles Douglas," *The Gentleman's and London Magazine: or Monthly Chronologer*, July, 1791 (London), pp. 359-360.

she would not inherit anything upon his death. Lydia proceeded to marry Bingham anyway.

The day after Douglas had written the letter to Helena, that same eldest daughter wrote a letter to Adam Smith asking for his assistance in her attempt to reconcile with Sir Charles. Unfortunately this was never to happen, since Douglas died such a short time later. The lawsuit she filed along with her husband to obtain a share of her father's estate was appealed all the way to the House of Lords, the equivalent of an American case reaching the United States Supreme Court. It had been decided by the Scottish courts that Lydia should receive her portion of Sir Charles' estate because under Scottish law a parent cannot control whom a child could or could not marry (the legal term being *contra libertatum matrimonii*). However, the case was appealed to the House of Lords on the grounds that Sir Charles was not a resident of Scotland, and that the case should be decided under English law, which would permit Lydia's disinheritance. The House of Lords determined that, since Sir Charles had not lived in Scotland since the age of twelve and had given up his original domicile upon entering into the foreign service, he had actually become a resident of England, and the codicil to his will was determined to be legal.

After Sir Charles' death, it was said in several periodicals of the time, including *Gentleman's Magazine,* "He was a very good, a very brave, and a very honest man."[1] One could easily add "very loyal" to that list of qualities. He always did his duty and served his commanders to the best of his ability, often going far beyond what was required of him in any given situation. As it stated in *A Biographical Dictionary of Eminent Scotsmen,* "...he left the character of a brave and admirable officer."[2]

---

[1] *The Naval Chronicle for 1805: Containing a General and Biographical History of the Royal Navy of the United Kingdom; with a Variety of Original Papers of Nautical Subjects* (London: I. Gold, 1805), p. 445. See also Hadden, p. 300 (footnote).

[2] Robert Chambers and Thomas Thomson. *A Biographical Dictionary of Eminent Scotsmen.* (Glasgow: Blackie and Son, 1855), p. 453.

CHAPTER NINE

THE BREAKING OF THE LINE CONTROVERSY

It is from the public having laboured under the error of believing, that the grand secret was disclosed, and taught, in "*the book*," that so much credit has been, hypothetically, ascribed to Mr. Clerk.

Sir Howard Douglas[1]

You have removed all doubt on the matter from my mind....This manoeuvre was one of the happiest ever introduced into naval warfare, and I think your duty leaves you but one course to pursue with those documents in your possession.

You must lay them before the public."

Sir Walter Scott to Sir Howard Douglas[2]

Years after Sir Charles Douglas died, a controversy arose over the origination of the breaking of the line maneuver. It had been generally accepted by the public that Admiral Rodney had come up with the brilliant idea of breaking the French line, and that

---

[1] Howard Douglas, *Naval Evolutions: A Memoir* (London: Thomas and William Boone, 1832.University of Michigan reprint under the Michigan Historical Reprint Series), p. 17.

[2] Fullom, p. 294.

credit for the victory was his. But there were other views. A Scot named John Clerk of Eldin, who had written an *Essay on Naval Tactics*, believed that Rodney had been aware of his book, including the idea on breaking the line that he presented in it, and indeed took credit for the celebrated maneuver in later editions. A version was even published posthumously in 1827 that contained notes by Lord Rodney himself, which many took to be proof of Clerk's claims.

Meanwhile, the family and friends of Sir Charles Douglas, as well as many naval officers and sailors, believed that it had been Douglas, not Rodney, who had the idea. The first time this is mentioned in print is probably in Admiral Ekin's *Naval Battles* in 1829:

> Of the character and talents of Sir Charles Douglas, then Captain of the fleet, the service at large cannot be ignorant; yet it may not generally be known, that to him, by passing through the enemy's line, are we indebted for the fortunate result of that day. Lord Rodney had at first opposed it, by directing the helm to be put to *starboard*, when Sir C. Douglas had ordered it to be put "*a-port*;" and the master, seeing the inconvenience likely to arise from this difference of opinion, caused the helm to be kept *a-mid-ships*; and soon after, Sir C. Douglas urging it a second time, the Chief said, "then do it as you please." The fault was in not doing more afterwards. [1]

Ekin also quoted the French naval researcher, Paul Hoste, and showed that he had discussed the breaking of the line maneuver well before Clerk did.

But it was not until Sir Charles' son, General Sir Howard Douglas, wrote his "Statement of Some Important Facts, Supported by Authentic Documents, Relating to the Operation of Breaking the Enemy's Line, as Practiced for the First Time in the Celebrated Battle of the 12th of April, 1782" as part of his *Treatise on Naval Gunnery* in 1829 that the controversy came to a head. [2] The *Quarterly Review*, a popular, conservative London magazine, published an ostensibly unbiased, but in reality quite one-sided, article taking to task both Sir Howard Douglas and the supporters

---

[1] Charles Ekin, *The Naval Battles of Great Britain* (London: Baldwin and Cradock, 1828), p. 176.

[2] Howard Douglas, *A Treatise on Naval Gunnery* (London: John Murray, Albemarle Street, 1860).

of the then-late Clerk of Eldin in its January 1830 issue. Shortly afterward, the *Edinburgh Review*, the liberal competition, published its own views on why Clerk should be credited. This was followed by Sir Howard defending himself and his evidence in the *United Service Journal*, a less-well-known military magazine, and in an entire book entitled *Naval Evolutions* in 1832. Noted naval expert Alfred T. Mahan said of Sir Howard's documentation, "...it may be said that the son of Sir Charles Douglas, Rodney's chief-of-staff, brought forward an amount of positive evidence, the only kind that could be accepted to diminish the credit of the person wholly responsible for the results, which proves that the suggestion came from Douglas, and Rodney's consent was with difficulty obtained." [1] Interestingly, the *Quarterly Review* article stated that Sir Howard's evidence obviously showed that Clerk had no claim to the maneuver, but disputed his claims against Rodney; while the *Edinburgh Review* said that Sir Howard's refutation of Rodney's claim was clearly proven, but that Douglas got the idea from Clerk.

Other journals and books came down on one of the three sides, the authors of many of which appear to have only read one or two of the previous works. The thing in common among those who support Clerk or Rodney is that they either leave out Sir Howard's evidence entirely, or ignore the later evidence in *United Service Journal* and *Naval Evolutions* and focus on the earlier controversy, dismissing Charles Dashwood's story. For example, in an 1852 book on gunnery, Colonel Francis Chesney credited Clerk and acknowledged the controversy regarding Rodney, but made no mention of Douglas. [2] It is no surprise, then, that he referenced Clerk's own book, Professor Playfair's biography of Clerk, the *Edinburgh Review*, and the *Quarterly Review*, and made no mention of the other available evidence. John Watkins wrote a lengthy defense of Clerk in an 1831 book about William IV. [3] *Biography, or Third Edition of "The English Encyclopedia" Vol. II* stated in 1867 that "...to Sir Charles Douglas has been ascribed, apparently with truth, the merit of suggesting the manoeuvre of breaking through

---

[1] Mahan, *Influence of Sea Power*, pp. 367-368.

[2] Col. Francis Rawdon Chesney, *Observations on the Past and Present State of Fire-Arms, and on the Probable Effects in War of the New Musket* (London: Longman, Brown, Green, and Longmans, 1852), p. 15.

[3] John Watkins, *The Life and Times of "England's Patriot King," William the Fourth: With a Brief Memoir of Her Majesty Queen Adelaide, and Her Family* (London: Fisher, Son & Jackson, 1831), pp. 74-78.

the centre of the French line of battle, and by this operation rendering some of the enemy's ships useless, and thus gaining the victory."[1] W.M. James' *The British Navy in Adversity,* published in 1933, mentions that "some pamphlets" were published giving credit to Douglas, but brings up the stories of Lords Cranstoun and Cumberland in order to reject those pamphlets.[2] The 1945 book by Charles Lee Lewis, *Admiral De Grasse and American Independence,* states that Douglas pointed the maneuver out to Rodney.[3] Even as recently as a few years ago, Arthur Herman gave credit to Douglas, but supposed that Rodney at first misunderstood him, then agreed once he realized what he was saying.[4]

Obviously, the controversy has never ended, and secondary sources have not been in any kind of agreement in the century and a quarter since the events occurred. To properly assess the claims, the evidence for all three versions should be thoroughly reviewed.

CLERK OF ELDIN

> "Seamanship...is an art. It is not something that can be picked up and studied in one's spare time; indeed, it allows one no spare time for anything else."
>
> Pericles[5]

John Clerk, Laird of Eldin, was not a sailor, but a merchant who had always had an interest in naval battles, even though he had actually been to sea very little. He did write about naval tactics and, in a pamphlet printed for friends in 1782, *An Enquiry on Naval Tactics,* (published publicly as *An Essay on Naval Tactics* in 1790), discussed his idea for breaking the line from the windward in naval battles. Whether or not his idea was known to Rodney, or was even the same as the tactic used at the Battle of the Saints, is a

---

[1] Charles Knight (ed.), *Biography, or Third Edition of "The English Encyclopedia"Vol. II* (London: Bradbury, Evans, & Co., 1867), p. 640.

[2] W.M. James, *The British Navy in Adversity: A Study of the War of American Independence* (London: Longmans, Green and Co., 1933), pp. 345-346.

[3] Charles Lee Lewis, *Admiral De Grasse and American Independence* (Baltimore: United States Naval Institute, 1945), p. 239.

[4] Arthur Herman, *To Rule the Waves: How the British Navy Shaped the Modern World,* (New York: Harper Perennial, 2004), pp. 317-318.

[5] Clark G. Reynolds, *Navies in History* (Annapolis: Naval Institute Press, 1998), p. 1.

matter of dispute, although Sir Howard Douglas' evidence against the possibility of their having any knowledge on the 12th of April leaves little doubt.

Clerk stated in the preface to a later edition in 1804 that he met with Rodney's secretary, Richard Atkinson, in 1780, and gave him notes and sketches regarding the maneuver to give to Rodney before he left for the West Indies. However, Sir Howard Douglas pointed out that Rodney first sailed for the West Indies in 1779, so there is no way Atkinson would have been able to give Rodney the documents or discuss the tactic before he left.[1] Later, in a biography of Clerk, Professor John Playfair repeated the claim that Clerk suggested his idea to associates of Lord Rodney prior to 1780, and alleged that Clerk also met with Sir Charles Douglas himself, which would mean that, regardless of who took the initiative on the 12th of April, the plan originated with him.[2] Yet, if Clerk had met with Douglas, he never mentioned it himself, and a facsimile of a letter from Douglas to his sister in 1783 was published in *Naval Evolutions*, and, in response to such rumors, stated that he never met with a "Mr. Clark," whom he thought was a naval officer.[3] Other witnesses onboard the *Formidable*, including Sir Gilbert Blane, Frederick Knight, and Joseph York, stated that they had never even heard Clerk's name until many years after the battle. Moreover, Playfair's attempt to fix the dates by stating that Douglas left for the West Indies several months after Rodney, and therefore could have relayed the information to him before the Battle of the Saints, is also demonstrably false. Rodney had returned for a short time in 1781, and both Rodney and Douglas left for the West Indies together on the 1st or 2nd of January 1782, within a day of Clerk's pamphlet being published.[4] Relatives of Lord Rodney vehemently denied that he had ever seen Clerk's

---

[1] *Quarterly* Review, pp. 52-53. See also Douglas, *Naval Evolutions*, pp. 9-10.

[2] John Playfair. "On the Naval Tactics of the Late John Clerk, Esq. of Eldin," *The Works of John Playfair*, Vol. III (Edinburgh: Archibald Constable & Co., 1822), p. 12.

[3] Douglas' sister, Helena Baillie was a well-known gossip in Edinburgh to the point where she was sued for slander by a neighbor, so she was probably well-versed in such rumors at the time. See Leah Leneman, "Defamation in Scotland, 1750-1800," *Continuity and Change*, Number 15 (United Kingdom: Cambridge University Press, 2000), pp. 209-234. See Appendix for an excerpt from the letter.

[4] *Quarterly Review*, p. 53. Some sources say January 1, others January 2.

book or met the man before 1782, and Sir Howard Douglas like-wise refuted any meetings between Clerk and his father. Further, Sir Howard had in his possession a copy of the version of Clerk's book printed before the battle in 1782, and stated unequivocally that it did not even present the specific method of breaking the line used on 12th April (from the leeward), as did the later version, which did not have any of Rodney's hand-written notes in that section because it was added later.[1]

Many observers were convinced by either the *Quarterly Review* or by Sir Howard that Clerk's claims were unfounded. A *London Times* article published in 1893 stated, "That John Clerk, of Eldin, had advocated it from the arm-chair before it was employed in the Battle of the Saints is a coincidence only."[2] In the third volume of his *Life of Napoleon Buonaparte*, originally published in 1827, Sir Walter Scott stated in a footnote: "John Clerk of Eldin; a name never to be mentioned by Britons without respect and veneration, since, until his systematic *Essay Upon Naval Tactics* appeared the breaking of the line (whatever professional jealousy may allege to the contrary) was never practiced on decided and defined principle."[3] And yet, when Sir Howard Douglas showed him his evidence to the contrary, Scott was not only convinced of his error, he even urged Sir Howard to make his evidence public.[4] This is especially noteworthy in that one of Sir Walter's best friends was William Clerk, the son of John Clerk.[5]

In 1789, seven years after the battle, a copy of Clerk's *Essay on Naval Tactics* was sent to Lord Rodney for his opinion on it. Rodney wrote copious notes in the margins, including the section on the breaking of the line from the windward maneuver, and yet never once mentioned anything regarding first reading about the maneuver there. In fact, Sir Howard Douglas proved that the section on breaking the line from the leeward did not even exist in the copy that Rodney annotated. Furthermore, as the editor of the *Quarterly Review* article noted, "We venture to say no one will

---

[1] Douglas, *Naval Evolutions*, pp. 6-10; Fullom, p. 293.

[2] "Sea Power," *Proceedings of the United States Naval Institute*. Annapolis, MD: U.S. Naval Institute, 1893. Reprinted from *London Times and Fortnightly Review*, p. 462.

[3] Sir Walter Scott, *Life of Napoleon Bonaparte*, Vol 3. (Edinburgh: A. & C. Black, 1873), p. 114.

[4] Fullom, p. 294.

[5] John Gibson Lockhart, *Memoirs of Sir Walter Scott* (London: MacMillan and Co., 1900), p. 50.

readily believe that Lord Rodney was capable of annotating thus deliberately on Clerk's book in 1789, if he had been conscious of owing the great victory of 1782 to its suggestions, without manfully and distinctly expressing his sense of his obligations in some part of his comments."[1]

Still, if one investigates the matter without digging past the surface materials, it may be difficult to find refutations of Clerk's defenders. Playfair's biography of Clerk was widely read, and he claimed on a reading tour that Clerk had been robbed of the credit for political reasons.[2] Historians and writers from Henry Lord Brougham in 1870 to David Gates today, and even recent History Channel programs on the Royal Navy, have continued to credit Clerk, either based on Playfair's claims, or a lack of knowledge of, or attention to, the plentiful evidence to the contrary.[3] In fact, a magazine called *Library World,* at the turn of the last century, went so far as to criticize a book on naval tactics for ignoring Clerk's "contribution."[4]

LORD RODNEY

The name Admiral George Brydges, Lord Rodney, may not enjoy the fame of Horatio Nelson, but to those familiar with British naval history he is ranked among such eminent officers as Lord Nelson himself. Rodney had a long and illustrious, albeit controversial, career in the Royal Navy. After being raised by wealthy relatives, he joined the navy at a very young age, and, through a

---

[1] *Id.*

[2] Letter from Lord Webb Seymour to his brother in Lady Guendolen Ramsden, *Correspondence of Two Brothers: Edward Adolphus, Eleventh Duke of Somerset, and His Brother, Lord Webb Seymour, 1800 to 1819 and After* (London: Longmans, Green and Co, 1906), p. 229.

[3] For examples, see Henry Lord Brougham, *The Life and Times of Henry Lord Brougham* (New York: Harper & Brothers, Publishers, 1871); David Gates, *Warfare in the Nineteenth Century.* (Hampshire, England: Palgrove, 2001); "Wooden Walls," *The Royal Navy,* Jason Markham and Monte Markham, producers (A&E Television Networks, 2002), Television program; "Great Ships: Ships of the Line," *The Royal Navy,* Monte Markham, producer and director (A&E Television Networks, 1996), Television program; "Clerk, John of Eldin," *Dictionary of National Biography,* Vol. XI, Leslie Stephens (ed.) (New York: MacMillan and Co., 1887);

[4] *Library World: A Medium of Intercommunication for Librarians,* Vol. VIII, July, 1905 to June, 1906 (London: Library Supply Co., 1906), p. 196.

combination of connections, good fortune, and merit, quickly moved up in rank. His naval career was a roller coaster, with great victories often overshadowed by poor health, nearly constant financial troubles due to a gambling problem, and assaults on his reputation by fellow officers at sea and politicians at home.[1] According to Pieter van der Merwe of the National Maritime Museum: "I don't know if you would have liked Rodney if you ever met him. He was extremely abrasive, arrogant, bold, hypochondriac, greedy."[2]

Despite such powerful detractors as the distinguished Admiral Sir Samuel Hood, there is little doubt that Rodney was one of the best naval commanders of his time. He was made one of the youngest captains in the fleet at the age of twenty-five, and six years later became governor of Newfoundland.[3] During the Seven Years War he was promoted to rear admiral, and, following a period of exile in Paris to avoid debtors, Rodney became commander-in-chief of the Leeward Islands (West Indies) in 1778. But it was during the period of 1779-1782 that he really distinguished himself. At the close of the American War for Independence, Rodney had captured or destroyed sixteen ships of the line in two and a half years, and captured the commanding admiral of each of the nations with which Britain was still at war.[4] The Saints was his final battle, and he retired upon his return home to England.

Rodney took at least his fair share of prizes and credit, including for the maneuver at the Battle of the Saints. He was known to be egotistical and self-serving, which sometimes made him unpopular with his officers. His difficulties with other officers included his captain of the fleet, Sir Charles Douglas.

As with Douglas, the controversy regarding who should be credited with the idea to break the French line at the Battle of the Saints arose after Rodney's death. Despite some modern historians' assertions that Clerk himself never actually claimed that Rodney's maneuver came from him, Clerk blatantly made the claim in the preface to his 1804 edition (reprinted in the 1827 edition) that Rodney had been influenced by his book, which had mentioned a

---

[1] Trew, pp. 2-4.

[2] *Voyages*, "Great Ships of the Line," (The History Channel, 1996).

[3] Trew, p. 15; Breen, p. 230.

[4] Breen, pp. 235-237, 245.

similar tactic.[1] Rodney's family and friends were outraged by this and quickly refuted the claim. But Sir Charles' son, Sir Howard, as well as most of the witnesses to the battle, stated that it was Sir Charles who not only suggested the maneuver to Rodney, but also had to argue with him about it almost to the point of insubordination. In *Naval Evolutions: a Memoir*, Sir Howard proved that the maneuver was nothing new in naval tactics, and was hardly invented by Clerk, Rodney, or Douglas, a fact supported by the discovery of the tactic mentioned in earlier Fighting Instructions and signal books that were part of the Graves Collection.[2] The remaining question would be whether Rodney broke the line of his own initiative, or whether the move was suggested by Douglas. The evidence produced by Sir Howard, especially the numerous firsthand accounts by eyewitnesses, overwhelmingly indicates the latter.

SIR CHARLES DOUGLAS

Although Sir Charles never publicly took credit for the breaking the line maneuver, it appears that this was simply a matter of loyalty, duty, and discretion on his part. *Distinguished Men of Modern Times* stated that "it is certain that the gallant and generous officer...rejected all praise which seemed to him in the least to derogate from the glory of his commanding officer."[3] Sir Gilbert Blane wrote that Douglas refused to accept any compliments to himself at the expense of Rodney, to the point of once telling a fellow dinner guest "to keep his breath to cool his porridge."[4] However, this should be taken more as an indication of Douglas' char-

---

[1] His exact words were "Sir George Rodney himself, when he arrived in Britain, made no scruple to acknowledge, that I had suggested the manoeuvres by which he had gained the victory of the 12th of April 1782." John Clerk, *An Essay on Naval Tactics, Systematical and Historical, with Explanatory Plates*, Third Edition (Edinburgh: Adam Black, 1827), preface.

[2] Robison, p. 346. It should be noted that Douglas was part of the Channel Fleet at the same time, and would have been well aware of the same Instructions, as was Commodore Affleck, who broke the line that day as well. See also Julian S. Corbett, *Signals and Instructions, 1776-1794* (London: Navy Records Society, 1908, Elibron Classics reprint, 2005), p.264.

[3] *Distinguished Men of Modern Times (in Four Volumes)*, Vol. III (London: Charles Knight & Co., 1888), p. 478.

[4] Mundy, *Rodney*, p. 305.

acter than any admission that he played no part in the maneuver. Furthermore, since he received no remuneration—money or honorary—from the British government despite the part he played in the victory, Douglas was completely dependent upon Rodney himself for any sort of reward.

It is noteworthy that credit *is* taken on his headstone at Greyfriars Church in Edinburgh, Scotland.[1] Whether this was the decision of a family member, a friend, or perhaps his own way of finally setting the matter straight is unknown. Sir Howard stated in a letter to the editors of *United Service Magazine* that Sir Charles accepted the congratulations of close friends and family for the victory in private, but secretly longed for the public acknowledgement given to his commander-in-chief, and "went to his grave with a spirit wounded and mortified by neglect, for splendid, but unrequited, services."[2]

While the question of Clerk's contribution can be fairly easily laid to rest by the evidence, the dispute between backers of Rodney and Douglas is not so easily resolved. Circumstantial evidence abounds on both sides. Both men were certainly tactical giants, with numerous victories on their records. But Douglas had the advantage with respect to "thinking outside the box." The fact that he rammed the *Isis* into the ice in order to sail up the St. Lawrence River and relieve Quebec during the Americans' siege of that city shows not only his ingenuity, but his willingness to embrace risk and try something unusual and untested. His confidence in his own ideas on naval gunnery led him to use his own money to change the cannons on *The Duke* from matches over to flintlocks, as well as the other changes discussed earlier.

Lord Rodney, on the other hand, had a habit of sticking to the rules, and admonishing those who did not. A.T. Mahan noted that Rodney was from the more cautious school of naval commanders, much like the French. He had two of the officers under his com-

---

[1] His memorial reads: "To the revered memory of Rear Admiral Sir Chas Douglas, Bart., Son of Chas Ayton Douglas of Kinglassie, Born 1727 Died 1789, a distinguished naval officer, he relieved Quebec 1778 and when Captain of the Fleet to Adl Sir George Rodney in the heat of battle first suggested the manoeuvre known as the breaking of the line, 12 April 1782. Interred beside his brother near this spot." National Maritime Museum, Greenwich (Internet: accessed online at http://www.nmm.ac.uk/memorials/Memorial.cfm?Search=douglas&MemorialID=M560)

[2] *United Service Journal and Naval Military Magazine, 1830 Part I,* London: Henry Colburn and Richard Bentley (1830), p. 355.

mand court-martialed following the Battle of Martinique in 1780 for not following his instructions to the letter. A memorandum of advice to his son, John (whom he had made a captain while John was still a teenager) begins: "The first consideration of a captain of a man of war is to be particularly attentive in perusing and studying the Sailing and Fighting Instructions he may receive from the Admiralty..." [1] And in his notes made in the margins of Clerk's book, he says, "The naval instructions want a thorough reformation; but 'tis not in the power of every commander-in-chief to make what additions he pleases." [2] It should also be mentioned that Rodney, as a newly-promoted rear-admiral, commanded the van of Admiral Mathews' fleet at the previously mentioned Battle of Toulan, and saw both his commander-in-chief and vice-admiral court-martialed for deviating from the Instructions. Obviously, it would have been no small matter for Rodney to depart from the Instructions by breaking the line, regardless of the circumstances at the time.

It was pointed out by British naval expert Sir Julian Corbett in *Signals and Instructions*, as well as American Rear-Admiral S.S. Robison in *A History of Naval Tactics*, that with the discovery of the Graves Collection, there is proof that a signal for breaking the line existed in the channel fleet before the Battle of the Saints. Robison stated that Rodney almost certainly knew of both the tactic and the signal, and that Douglas definitely did, having just previously been a part of that fleet. Therefore, the subject of adding a signal for breaking the line was surely discussed, and so must have been rejected by Rodney. [3] If he was planning on using the tactic beforehand as his defenders claimed, then one has to wonder why he would not have added the signal and informed his captains. Corbett was even more emphatic, stating evidence that Rodney probably knew about the signal for breaking the line (or "crossing the T") as far back as 1779, since Admiral Kempenfelt added it to the signal book before Rodney first went to the West Indies. He went on to point out that,

> In any case he must have known of it when he went out the second time in 1782, for he took with him Sir Charles Douglas, who had been commanding the Duke 98 in the Channel during the whole period of Kempenfelt's ascendancy. As a senior captain and the admiral's second astern,

---

[1] Trew, p. 200.

[2] Douglas, *Naval Evolutions*, Appendix I, p. b.

[3] Robison, pp. 347-348; Corbett, p. 264.

Douglas must have been perfectly familiar with Kempenfelt's ideas and it was natural enough he should urge the Channel manoeuvre upon Rodney when he saw a chance for it in the crisis of the action off the Saints. [1]

He concluded his argument by enumerating the case in this way: (1) the signal for breaking the line was in the Channel Book at the time of the Battle of the Saints; (2) the same signal was *not* in Rodney's signal book at that time; (3) the two officers responsible for the maneuver at the Saints (Douglas and Affleck) were both "Channel men;" and (4) the man who recorded the signal in the Channel Book in the first place (Thomas Graves) was Affleck's flag captain at the time of the battle.

It has been suggested by some, such as the writer in the *Quarterly Review* (Sir John Barrow), Rodney's biographer (and son-in-law) General Godfrey Mundy, and W. H. Adams, that Rodney apparently attempted to break the French line during an earlier battle off Martinique. [2] Although Rodney's flagship, the *Sandwich*, did end up on the other side of the French line (by itself), the notion that this was intentional is most likely inaccurate, and even if it were, it would not automatically fall on his side of the argument. Many analysts, including Corbett, believe Rodney was simply trying to concentrate his fire upon a small part of the opposing line (in this case, center and the rear) rather than cut the line with his own, as was done in the later battle. [3] This corresponds with Rodney's letters and notes concerning the battle and his intentions. Nowhere does Rodney indicate that he intended to break the line or went through the gap on purpose, including his notes on the battle in Clerk's book. Corbett points to the fact that the only signals Rodney took from Kempenfelt were those for attacking the van, center, or rear, and not the one for breaking the line. In any case, the attempt was not successful at Martinique due to the failure of some of Rodney's officers to follow his signals. Because of his personality, Rodney often had difficulty relaying his wishes to his officers, and in this case, it resulted in two of his own captains being court-martialed. If anything, this may be seen as yet another reason why Rodney would have been hesitant to attempt a similar maneuver again two years later, fearing a similar outcome.

---

[1] Corbett, *Signals*, p. 121.

[2] See *Quarterly Review*, p. 78; Mundy, p. 295-297; Adams, p. 159.

[3] Trew, p. 182.

Another factor to take into consideration is Rodney's poor health. By all accounts, the admiral was extremely ill, and spent most of the day in his cabin. Before leaving for the West Indies, "His gout had returned on him so cruelly at Plymouth that he had been compelled to leave the very signing of his letters to Sir Charles Douglas."[1] Rodney's physician, Gilbert Blane, wrote in a memoir that

> ...it was considered as a fortunate circumstance for the service, that the Commander-in-Chief of the fleet in the West Indies, in the memorable campaign of 1782, should have had about his person to assist and advise him, so able an officer as Sir Charles Douglas, he himself being almost always in such bad health, either from illness or from convalescence from the gout, from debility and unequal spirits, so as to render him less equal to the fatiguing and anxious duties inseparable from such high responsibility.[2]

Some crew members would go so far as to report that Rodney spent most of the Battle of the Saints sitting in a chair.[3]

Hearsay evidence exists on both sides. Friends of Lord Rodney claimed that Douglas had admitted that Rodney first had the idea. One associate, the writer Richard Cumberland, even stated that Douglas told him he had tried to talk Rodney out of breaking the line after Rodney ordered it.[4] Cumberland mentioned that Rodney chided Sir Charles for being insubordinate, and Sir Charles was later upset about his admiral's refusal to follow his advice. It is possible, perhaps even probable, that Cumberland was confusing the argument between Rodney and Douglas that resulted in the breaking of the French line with Douglas' later frustration at Rodney's refusal to chase the French fleet. This confusion is backed up by the fact that Cumberland attributed an exclamation during the battle ("Behold, the Greeks and Trojans contending for the body of Petroclus!") to Sir Charles, even though Sir Gilbert Blane, a witness to the actual event, said that the speech was made by Rodney following the breaking of the line. Rodney's supposed response to Sir Charles' "objection" to breaking the line was that his "counsel

---

[1] Hannay, p. 173.

[2] *United Service Journal and Naval Military Magazine, 1830 Part 1* (London: Henry Colburn and Richard Bentley, 1830, Compilation), p. 598.

[3] *Id.*

[4] *Ibid.*, p. 93.

was not called for; he required obedience only—he did not want advice."[1] Once again, another witness to the actual events, Sir Frederick Thesiger, attributed nearly the exact same quote to Rodney in response to Sir Charles pushing him to pursue the French fleet following the battle. In fact, Thesiger claims Sir Charles nearly resigned because of the incident. It should also be noted that Cumberland was quite old when he wrote the account, and advanced age was something that defenders of Rodney expected to be taken into consideration when reviewing the testimony of those witnesses who supported Douglas.

Further, Sir Howard Douglas stated that, even if that story were true, it merely served to illustrate Sir Charles' dedication to his commander-in-chief and his strong belief that it was his duty not to undermine his superior in public. Admiral Sir Samuel Hood, who was Rodney's second in command at the Battle of the Saints, claimed that Douglas was too fearful of Rodney to have made such a suggestion, but he was aboard his own ship, the *Barfleur*, at the time, so it was only supposition. Hood had a reputation for being highly critical of others, to the point that David Hannay, editor of the collection of his papers, stated, "Indeed, it is rarely that he has a good word for anybody, or that his criticism is not pointed by contempt."[2]   His harsh opinion of Douglas may have been partly a result of his disappointment in Rodney for not chasing and destroying the rest of the French fleet on the 12th of April, since he also (unfairly) blamed Douglas for this lapse in initiative.[3] Hood's opinion of Douglas is based on his mistaken belief that Douglas was afraid to argue with his admiral, when, in fact, witnesses indicate otherwise. It appears that Hood mistook Douglas' strict code of honor and refusal to speak against Rodney to another officer (Hood) for cowardice, when in reality Douglas merely had better manners and more self-control. On the other hand, even if it were true that Hood *was* correct about Douglas' reticence toward Rodney, it would also be another reason for Sir Charles not taking credit for the maneuver later on, even if it had been his idea.

---

[1] Adams, p. 158.

[2] Hannay, *Hood*, Vol. III, p. xiii.

[3]   Michael Duffy, "Samuel Hood, First Viscount Hood." *Precursors of Nelson: British Admirals of the Eighteenth Century*, Richard Harding and Peter LeFevre, eds. (Mechanicsburg, PA: Stockpole Books, 2000), p. 262.

In 1830, following several first-hand accounts (related below), Sir Howard Douglas produced a "Second Class of Evidence," which were letters addressed to Sir Charles "expressly ascribing to him the Manoeuvre in question, and congratulating him on the glory he had gained."[1] These letters came from such important men as Lords Howe, Sandwich, and Keppel.

Next, Sir Howard published what he called his "Third Class of Evidence," a number of letters from officers still living at the time, who were not on the *Formidable* during the battle but were in the fleet, that "prove that the belief and impression were general, if not universal, in the Fleet at the time, that my Father suggested, proposed, and urged the decisive, supermeditated operation."[2]

Finally, Sir Howard's "Fourth Class of Evidence" consisted of three "letters from officers who were at Jamaica when the fleet and prizes arrived, a few days after the action, to show the belief and impression were generally circulated and entertained in all societies at Port Royal that the decisive operation was pointed out by my Father at the important moment."[3] The third and fourth classes of evidence thoroughly contradict Captain Thomas White's claim in his *Naval Researches* that he doubted the claims about Douglas, and that he never heard anything mentioned within the fleet about Douglas arguing with Rodney.[4]

First hand accounts of what transpired aboard the *Formidable* tend to be detailed and one-sided. As mentioned earlier, Rodney took credit for the idea, but it is generally accepted that such was his personality that he would done so either way, while Douglas was mostly silent on the matter out of respect for his admiral and the chain of command. Further, since Douglas did not, like Rodney and Hood, receive his due from the British government (as noted earlier), he was dependent upon Rodney's generosity for any reward following the battle. So one must, as in a court of law, assess the testimony of eyewitnesses who were present at the time.

---

[1] *United Service Journal*, p. 599.

[2] *Ibid.*, p. 600.

[3] *Ibid.*, p. 602.

[4] Thomas White, *Naval Researches; or a Candid Inquiry into the Conduct of Admirals Byron, Graves, Hood and Rodney, in the Actions off Grenada, Chesapeak, St. Christophers, and of the Ninth and Twelfth of April, 1782* (Boston: Gregg Press, 1972), p. 109. White was a lieutenant aboard Hood's ship, the *Barfleur*, at the time. One of the main purposes of his book is to refute Clerk's claims, but in the process he is staunchly in Rodney's camp, and an even greater supporter of Hood.

Perhaps the most compelling evidence of all is the letter from Sir Charles Dashwood quoted earlier. In the article, Dashwood's letter is followed by an extract of the diary of Vice-Admiral Sir Joseph Sydney Yorke, who was also an *aide-de-camp* to Rodney and Douglas at the time. In Yorke's version, which is very close to Dashwood's, Douglas urged the admiral to break the line, to which Rodney replied that "it was a very hazardous experiment." The argument over turning the ship is also present in Yorke's diary, with Sir Charles repeatedly calling out to the helm to "luff."[1]

The *Quarterly Review's* editor (signed only "ART," but generally understood to be Sir John Barrow, Lord of the Admiralty) was not persuaded by Dashwood's or Yorke's testimony, and was actually quite cruel in his assessment.[2] He stated that Dashwood was too young at the time and it was too long ago for him to remember it so clearly, took issue with the timing and the background noise that must have existed, and even went so far as to ridicule some of the descriptions of the action.

With regard to the background noise, in a statement about the closeness of the ships, a French witness aboard the *Northumberland,* stated that he could hear the commands of the British officers.[3] If the sailors on enemy ships could hear the officers, then certainly an *aide-de-camp* standing next to them would not have had any trouble. After seeing the *Quarterly Review* article, Dashwood wrote a letter to the editor of the *United Service Journal,* in which he said his letter to Sir Howard Douglas "is canvassed with no small degree of acrimony" in that article and went on to defend and explain himself.[4] In that same issue of *United Service Journal,* Sir Howard pulled out all the stops and published many more accounts that backed up his claims and, specifically, Dashwood's letter.

Charles Thesiger, brother to Sir Frederick Thesiger (Rodney's first *aide-de-camp* on the *Formidable*), produced a letter that Frederick wrote to him at the time, in which he gave an account that not only supported Dashwood and Yorke's stories, but stated, "Sir Charles Douglas is the man who had the sole merit of fighting the *Formidable,*" and that he (Thesiger) had even disobeyed Rodney's direct order to turn the ship to starboard, since he was re-

---

[1] *Quarterly Review,* pp. 65-66.

[2] Trew, p. 178; *Quarterly Review,* pp. 66-79.

[3] Trew, p. 158.

[4] *United Service Journal,* p. 352-353.

quired to always obey the *last* order given, and Douglas continued to shout, "Luff, my boys, luff!" [1] If anyone had any reason to believe that Thesiger wrote the letter out of acrimony between him and Rodney, it should be noted that Rodney wrote him a glowing letter of recommendation to the Russian ambassador when Thesiger was looking for service in Catherine the Great's navy. [2]

The next letter printed in the *United Service* article was from Frederick Knight, who was Sir Charles Douglas' secretary at the time of the battle, and whose job was to record everything that happened. Knight also tells an almost identical story to the others, and states in no uncertain terms "that bold and fortunate manoeuvre rests wholly on the late Sir Charles Douglas!" [3] In another letter, Captain G. W. Blaney, a midshipman on the *Formidable* during the battle, states, "There can be no doubt of an altercation between the Commander-in-Chief and Captain of the Fleet, whether the helm should be put a-starboard or port, which was alternately done, and even a-port by the motion of Sir Charles' hand." A statement similar to the others' follows this, with Douglas calling, "luff, my man, luff" over Rodney's objections, and Rodney finally saying, "Do as you please, Sir Charles." Blaney wrote this letter with his journal, written the day after the battle, in front of him. [4]

One could certainly speculate, as the *Quarterly Review* did, as to why so many eyewitnesses would act in collusion to make up a story like Dashwood's. But without any known reason to doubt their statements, and their versions having been told at such disparate times and under such different circumstances, it would be an odd endeavor, and certainly one undertaken with some sort of ulterior motives.

Sir Archibald Alison, in his *History of Europe from the Commencement of the French Revolution in 1789 to the Restoration of the Bourbons in 1815*, put forth the theory that Rodney himself may, indeed, have begun telling people he had read Clerk before the Battle of the Saints, except not to give Clerk credit, but rather to further the claim that he had the maneuver in mind

---

[1] *United Service Journal*, pp. 596-597.

[2] *Naval Chronicle*, p. 445.

[3] *Ibid.*, p. 597.

[4] *Ibid.*, p. 598.

beforehand.[1] This would take the credit for its execution away from Douglas and place it back on Rodney.

Finally, there is another assertion that should be examined based on what is known about Rodney's character. Nathan Miller states that in the debate over credit for breaking the line, "inasmuch as he would have borne the blame had it failed, he is entitled to the credit."[2] However, assuming the version told by Dashwood, Yorke, and the others is truthful, Rodney would have had very little to lose by finally allowing Douglas to steer the *Formidable* into the French line. If the maneuver proved to be a success, which it did, he would receive and accept the credit for the victory, which he was only too happy to do. But if it failed, Rodney had many witnesses who overheard Douglas countermanding his orders several times, which certainly would have been grounds for a court martial. Rodney had ensured courts martial for his subordinates before, and he surely would have called for one again in such an event. Either way, Rodney would probably come through the matter unscathed. As with so many things in life, the people at the top tend to find a scapegoat for the bad, and take the credit and praise for the good.

---

[1] Sir Archibald Alison, *History of Europe from the Commencement of the French Revolution in 1789 to the Restoration of the Bourbons in 1815.* Ninth Edition, Vol. III. (Edinburgh: William Blackwood and Sons, 1854), p. 129.

[2] Miller, *Broadsides*, p. 95.

Rear-Admiral Sir Charles Douglas, 1st Baronet of Carr
(*Courtesy of Wikimedia Commons*) - Mezzotint by John Jones after the portrait by Henry Singleton (1791).

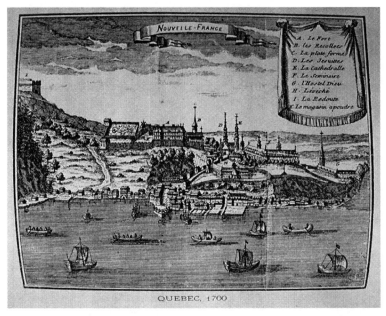

Quebec City, circa 1700

The St. Lawrence River was not considered navigable by warships until Douglas found some French pilots who assisted General Wolfe's British forces in the attack on Quebec in 1759, completely surprising the French under General Montcalm.

John Montague, 4th Earl of Sandwich

(*Courtesy of Wikimedia Commons*) - Sandwich was First Lord of the Admiralty throughout most of the American Revolutionary War, and sent Douglas to relieve Quebec and command the British Naval forces on the St. Lawrence.

Champlain Valley, 1777

Lake Champlain was the key to invading the American colonies from Canada, but Benedict Arnold had built a small flotilla to defend the lake from a British invasion.

General Sir Guy Carleton (Later Lord Dorchester)

(*Courtesy of Wikimedia Commons*) Carleton was the Governor of Canada at the time of the American Revolution, and was commander-in-chief of the forces on Lake Champlain at the Battle of Valcour Island.

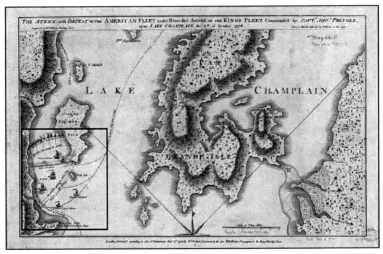

Valcour Island (Overview)

Valcour Island is located just off the western coast of Lake Champlain, and Arnold's forces hid in the small strait in between prior to the battle.

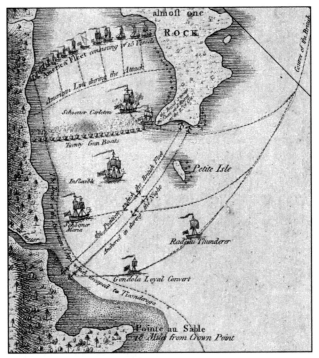

Valcour Island (Detail)

Although the British were victorious over Arnold's small fleet, the Americans managed to stall Carleton long enough to prevent the taking of Fort Ticonderoga until the following spring.

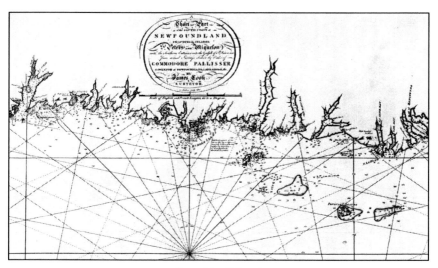

Cook's Chart

Captain James Cook was able to survey St. Pierre and Miquelon thanks to Douglas' ability to stall the French governor and settlers who arrived to occupy the islands.

Battle of Ushant, 1778

(*Courtesy of Wikimedia Commons*) The First Battle of Ushant was basically a draw, and led to the courts martial of Admiral Keppel and Vice-Admiral Hugh Palliser following public accusations of one another.

Admiral Augustus, Viscount Keppel

(*Courtesy of Wikimedia Commons*) Keppel was exonerated at his court martial following the Battle of Ushant, thanks in part to the testimony of Sir Charles Douglas

A Typical Naval Gun

While in the Channel Fleet, Douglas made many modifications to the guns aboard his ship, the *Duke*, mostly at his own expense.

A Flintlock Mechanism

(*Courtesy of Wikimedia Commons*) Douglas used his own money to change the guns on the *Duke* from matches over to flintlocks, and later did the same for the *Formidable* and other ships in Rodney's fleet. Their effectiveness at the Battle of the Saints helped convince the Admiralty to adopt them for the entire fleet.

The Battle of the Saints, 12 April 1782
Surrender of the Ville de Paris, by Thomas Whitcombe

(*Courtesy of Wikimedia Commons*) The Battle of the Saints was a great victory, re-establishing Britain as the world's premiere naval power and changing the way the British fought naval battles until end of the Age of Sail.

Admiral Sir George Brydges, Lord Rodney

(*Courtesy of Wikimedia Commons*) Rodney was the commander-in-chief at the Battle of the Saints and took credit for the breaking of the line maneuver, although many eyewitnesses stated that Douglas not only had the idea, but had to argue with Rodney to convince him to allow the maneuver.

A Scale Model of the *Formidable*

(*Courtesy of Wikimedia Commons*) The *Formidable* was Rodney's flagship during the Battle of the Saints, with Sir Charles Douglas on board as the captain-of-the-fleet.

Vice-Admiral Sir Samuel (Later Lord) Hood

(*Courtesy of Wikimedia Commons*) Hood was Rodney's second in command at the Battle of the Saints, and was very critical of both Rodney and Douglas following the battle.

General Sir Howard Douglas, 3rd Baronet of Carr

(*Personal family collection*) In the 1830s, Sir Charles' son, Sir Howard Douglas, engaged in a war of words over the credit for the breaking of the line maneuver, which eventually led to the publication of a book on the subject, entitled *Naval Evolutions: A Memoir*.

John Clerk of Eldin

(*Courtesy of Wikimedia Commons*) Clerk and his supporters believed Rodney's idea for breaking the line came from a pamphlet entitled *An Essay on Naval Tactics* that he had published in 1782.

Letter from Sir Charles Douglas to his sister, Helena Baillie

(From *Naval Evolutions* by Sir Howard Douglas) This letter, in which Douglas denies any knowledge of John Clerk (whom he thought was a naval officer at the time), was part of the evidence presented by Sir Howard Douglas in his book.

CHAPTER TEN

LEGACY

[Sir Howard Douglas] is an officer of first-rate ability and scientific attainments... his high talents and zeal in the service of his country were hereditary; to his own knowledge the distinguished merits of Sir Howard's father—Sir Charles Douglas, to whom the naval service of the country was greatly indebted—had not met their commensurate reward..."

His Majesty, King William IV
at the Royal Military College
at Sandhurst, June 1834.[1]

In addition to his own illustrious career in the Royal Navy, Sir Charles Douglas influenced the careers of many other important officers. As mentioned previously, he was instrumental in advancing the career of Edward Pellew following the Battle of Valcour Island, and Richard Dacres, whom he placed in command of the *Carleton* for that battle, went on to become an admiral as well. Sir Davidge Gould, his first lieutenant on the *Formidable*, went on to distinguish himself as a captain at the Battle of the Nile under Nelson, and died Vice-Admiral of the United Kingdom. Douglas was responsible for Samuel Greig becoming part of the Russian Navy, and one of its greatest admirals. His testimony at the court martial of Keppel helped to vindicate the admiral, who went on to become

---

[1] Fullom, pp. 314-15.

First Lord of the Admiralty. Without Douglas' assistance, advice, and gunnery innovations, it can certainly be argued that Rodney's victory over the French at the Saints may not have been so great, if it had even been a victory at all. Without that victory, Rodney would have simply been replaced by Piggott and returned home in disgrace. Furthermore, the breaking of the line maneuver became standard practice in the Royal Navy, including by Nelson at the Battles of the Nile and Trafalgar. But just as important to the victories of the British in the Napoleonic Wars and the Royal Navy's ascendancy in the Nineteenth Century were the changes made to naval gunnery as a result of Sir Charles' influence.

The Baronetcy of Carr lasted until the death of Major Sir James Stewart Douglas, 6th Baronet, in 1940. It was first passed on to Sir Charles' eldest son, William-Henry Douglas, who was with his father at the Battle of the Saints. He had been made a post-captain and placed in command of the French ship *Glorieux* at the age of only twenty, on 15 April 1782, three days after it was captured in the battle, then became captain of the frigate *Licorne*, 32 guns, later that year. William-Henry was promoted to rear admiral of the white himself in 1804, and rear admiral of the red in 1805. He eventually surpassed his father's highest rank when he became vice-admiral of the blue, and was even one of only six admirals carrying the canopy at Lord Nelson's funeral. William died at the age of forty-nine at the Royal Hospital in Chelsea in 1809 "after a long and painful illness."[1] Because William was unmarried and childless, and his next brother, Charles, another naval captain, died soon afterward, Howard became the 3rd Baronet.

As a young boy, Charles' son, Howard, idolized his father, and wanted to join the navy. But after Sir Charles' death, the young Howard was instead steered toward a military academy and the army. Sir Howard became an artillery expert himself, and despite rising to the rank of general in the British Army, eventually invented some improvements to naval gunnery and wrote a *Treatise on Naval Gunnery*, which was respected by the navy, approved by the Admiralty, and became a textbook on naval gunnery for many years.

General Sir Howard Douglas grew up dreaming of being a naval officer like his father and older brothers. His biographer

---

[1] *The Scots Magazine and Edinburgh Literary Miscellany*, Vol. LXXI (Edinburgh: Archibald Constable and Company, 1809), p. 478.

claimed that in 1789, his father came home to take the thirteen-year-old Howard along with him to serve on his ship when Sir Charles suddenly died of apoplexy during the celebrations for King George III's recovery from a grave illness. Howard's guardians thought it better that he attend the military academy at Woolwich instead of going into the navy, but that did not stop Howard from learning to sail on local fishing vessels whenever he could get away from his schoolwork.

Despite graduating as a lieutenant in the artillery, Howard did get the opportunity to act as a sailor on several occasions, including in 1796, while serving in Canada. When the Canadian government needed to send a vessel to gather intelligence on the actions of a French admiral, there were no naval officers available to command it. They discovered that Douglas had a small sailing boat of his own, and a rumor had begun that he had previously served in the navy. He was asked to command the cruiser that was being sent to gather intelligence, and he gladly accepted. He also acted as first mate on a merchant vessel on which he traveled back to England when one of his brothers had died in 1799.

But his real area of expertise was artillery, and soon after returning to England, now-Major Douglas became an instructor at the Royal Military College at High Wycombe. He had inherited his father's obsession with gunnery as well as his ingenuity, and he set about studying everything he could on the subject, including spherical geometry and spherical trigonometry, nautical astronomy, and the theorems for the laws of navigation, projection of spheres, and construction of maps, as well as plane, rhomb, and great-circle sailing. He became so familiar with using a sextant and repeating circle that he invented his own, simplified version, which he called the Improved Reflecting Circle and Semi-circle for land and marine surveying. Otherwise known as a "reflecting alidade," it was especially useful for military surveying.[1] Scientists and others were so impressed with the combined reflection circle-protractor that he was soon after elected to the Royal Society. After a stint in the Peninsular War, Douglas (now a colonel) also proposed a new type of double flintlock for cannons, which could easily be rotated if one side failed during the heat of battle. The Royal Navy adopted these in 1818.

---

[1] "Alidade (reflecting)," Smithsonian Institute National Museum of American History [online]; Internet: available at http://american history. si.edu/collections/surveying/object.cfm?record number=764354

Even more than his actual inventions, Sir Howard's writings on naval gunnery greatly contributed to the subject. He first wrote about his thoughts on naval gunnery in 1817, not to be published, but to present his important ideas to the Admiralty. His fear was that naval officers would be offended that a soldier felt he could offer solutions to problems at sea, despite the facts that his father had been a famous admiral, that he was himself known as one of the most scientifically gifted soldiers in the Army, and was now the superintendent of the Royal Military Academy.

Having observed naval operations throughout the Napoleonic Wars, he strongly believed the navy had actually lost much of its strength since the time of the American Revolution, mostly due to overconfidence and the fact that gunners were no longer being properly trained and drilled. While many felt that the British Navy was invincible because it was so superior to its enemies at the time, Douglas thought otherwise. His argument was that these foreigners would be working extra hard to find ways to out-think and out-gun the Royal Navy, while the British rested on their laurels and became slack.

His first chapter deals with suggestions for remedying the problem, including the rotation of officers at gunnery classes for several weeks at a time, and the establishment of several depots of instruction for the training of gunners. Part II is about the theory and science of gunnery, and spends a great deal of time discussing windage, which was a major problem with all the guns in use at the time except the Carronade, as well as the effects of air friction on shot distance. Part III covers the manual on naval gunnery. Part IV is about the equipment, practice, and service of naval ordnance, and discusses such subjects as moisture in powder and rust on shot. Finally, Part V is on recent naval operations and tactics. Also included are many tables, charts, and diagrams.

Unfortunately, Sir Howard had only one connection at the Admiralty, Sir Graham Moore, and he was not very influential. Despite Sir Graham's efforts, most of the Board put off reading the *Treatise* for months, and Sir Howard began to think nothing would come of it. Then, a naval officer who had somehow read a copy of some of Douglas' essay attempted to pass the ideas off as his own, only to be tactfully rebutted by Sir Graham. But this worried Sir Howard, and he immediately requested that the Admiralty allow him to publish his essay as a book, for which they gave their permission. He hoped that the public would see the importance of, and embrace, his ideas, and that the backlash from the naval community would not be too harsh.

He published his essay as *A Treatise on Naval Gunnery* in 1819, and the reaction was the opposite of what he expected. The general public all but ignored the book, but naval officers who read it became his biggest supporters. Still, nothing was done on the Admiralty's part, and Douglas, now a Major General, went back to Canada to become Governor of New Brunswick. By the time of the second edition in 1829, the book was being used as a textbook on naval gunnery both in England and in other countries, but the Admiralty still had not put most of his ideas to use.

It was not until 1830, while Douglas was in the Netherlands to discuss the border dispute with Maine with the Dutch King (who was the arbitrator), that the Admiralty finally began to put into place the ideas set forth in the *Treatise*. Apparently, the French and other foreign governments had begun plans to implement some of his ideas, so some captains in the Royal Navy began pressuring the Admiralty to do the same.

The first gunnery instruction depot to be established was on board the *Excellent*, formerly the ship of Lord Collingwood, and the implementation of some of Douglas' other ideas followed. His book became a textbook on naval gunnery that influenced thousands of naval officers and seamen, not only in England but around the world.

In 1851, he published a third edition of the *Treatise*, and following the publication of *Naval Warfare Under Steam* in 1858, his final version of the *Treatise* was released in 1860.

Sir Howard's knowledge of naval gunnery also led to him offering his expertise when it came to whether the British Navy should adopt iron ships, or simply use plating over wooden ships. Sir Robert Peel solicited his opinion on the matter in 1848, and he was against the ironclads. The government took his advice and dropped the idea for the time being.

But, shortly before Douglas' death, the matter arose once again. This led to a war of words with Scott Russell, the man who built and designed the *Great Eastern*. Douglas was very much against ships with all-iron hulls, and believed iron armor should be placed over wooden hulls. He strongly felt that it was much more important to develop more effective gunnery. He also had seen the tests done with iron hulls at Woolwich and other places, and they showed that armor plating over a wooden hull was better at stopping shot than iron hulls. This time he lost the argument, and the Navy went on to build iron ships from then on.

The importance of Sir Charles Douglas in the saving of Quebec and to the British cause in the American Revolution, as well as his lasting contributions to naval gunnery, cannot be underestimated. His introduction of flintlocks and other innovations not only helped Admiral Rodney win his decisive victory at the Battle of the Saints, but also played a part in the long string of British victories that followed, including Nelson's enormous triumph at Trafalgar. His relative obscurity in the annals of naval history is proof that his career and ideas have, as King William IV said, "not met their commensurate reward."

APPENDIX A
Naval Career Timeline

- 1740 Joined Royal Navy at age twelve
- 1745 Midshipman at Siege of Louisbourg
- 1747 Past-Midshipman on HMS *Centurion*
- 1749 Served in Dutch Navy as a lieutenant
- 1753 Lieutenant in the Royal Navy
- 1759 Promoted to Commander, HMS *Boscawen,*16 guns
- 1761 Made Post-Captain; Commander of HMS *Unicorn*, 28 guns
- 1762 Commander of HMS *Syren*, 20 guns, Newfoundland
- 1764 Commander of HMS *Tweed*, 32 Guns
- 1764 Rear-Admiral in Russian Navy
- 1767 Commander of HMS *Emerald*, 32 guns
- 1770 Commander of HMS *St. Albans*, 61 guns
- 1774 Commander of HMS *Ardent*, 61 guns
- 1775 Commander of HMS *Isis*, 50 guns, Quebec
- 1776 Commodore in charge of St. Lawrence Fleet, building Lake Champlain fleet
- 1777 Commander of HMS *Stirling Castle*, 64 Guns, Channel Fleet
- 1778 Commander of HMS *Duke*, 98 guns, Channel Fleet
- 1781 Captain-of-the-Fleet of Sir George Rodney, HMS *Formidable*, West Indies

- 1783 Commodore and Commander-in-Chief of North American Station, HMS *Assistance*, 50 guns, HMS *Hermione*, 32 guns
- 1787 Promoted to Rear-Admiral
- 1789 Commander-in-Chief of North American Station, HMS *London Man*, 50 guns

APPENDIX B

LETTERS RELATING TO THE BREAKING OF THE LINE BATTLE OF THE SAINTS, 12 APRIL 1782

Reprinted from Sir Howard Douglas, *Naval Evolutions: A Memoir Containing a Review and Refutation of the Principal Essays and Arguments Advocating Mr. Clerk's Claims, in Relation to the Manoeuvre of the 12ᵗʰ of April 1782; and Vindicating, by Tactical Demonstration, and Numerous Authentic Documents, the Professional Skill of the British Officers Chiefly Concerned on that Memorable Occasion.* London: Thomas and William Boone, 1832.

Copy of a Letter from Captain Sir Charles Dashwood, K.C.B., etc.

Torquay, July 8, 1829.

DEAR SIR,

I AM very much obliged for the trouble you have taken in forwarding me the various documents, (which I herewith return,) relative to the glorious battle of the 12th of April, because, if I cannot throw any new light on this interesting subject, I can, at all events, corroborate the statement made by Admiral Ekins. Whether Sir George Rodney, or Sir Charles Douglas, had any conversation with Mr. Clerk previous to their leaving England, relative to the practicability of breaking an enemy's line; or whether these great and gallant officers ever conversed or consulted together on such a subject, is impossible for me to say; but I think I can sufficiently prove from circumstances that eventually occurred, and which came within my own knowledge, the absolute improbability of such a conversation having occurred with Mr. Clerk, or, that the Admiral and Captain of the Fleet had previously consulted together on the important subject; but, that the idea emanated from the mind of your excellent Father, in the hour of battle. I shall simply relate facts, to which I was an eye witness, and can vouch for their truth. Being one of the aide-de-camps to the Commander-in-Chief on that memorable day, it was my duty to attend both on him and the Captain of the Fleet, as occasion might require. It so happened, that some time after the battle had commenced, and whilst we were warmly engaged, I was standing near Sir Charles Douglas, who was leaning on the hammocks, (which in those days were stowed across the fore part of the quarter-deck,) his head resting on one hand, and his eye occasionally glancing on the enemy's line, and apparently in deep meditation, as if some great event was crossing his mind: suddenly raising his head, and turning quickly round, said, "Dash! where's Sir George?" "In the after cabin, Sir," I replied. He immediately went aft; I followed; and on meeting Sir George coming from the cabin close to the wheel, he took off his cocked hat with his right hand, holding his long spyglass in his left, making a low and profound bow, said, "Sir George, I give you joy of the victory!" "Poli!" said the Chief, as if half angry, 1' the day is not half won yet. "Break the line, Sir George!" said your Father, "the day is your own, and I will insure you the victory." "No," said the Admiral, "I will not break my line." After another request and another refusal, Sir Charles desired the helm to be put a-port; Sir George ordered it to starboard. On your Father ordering it again to port, the Admiral sternly said, "Remember, Sir Charles, that I am Commander in Chief: starboard, sir,"addressing the Master, who, during this controversy, had placed the helm amidships. Both the Admiral and Captain then separated; the former going aft, and the latter forward. In the course of a couple of minutes or so, each turned and again met nearly on the same spot, when Sir Charles quietly and coolly again addressed the Chief, "Only break the line, Sir George, and the day is your own." The Admiral then said, in a quick and hurried way, "Well, well, do as you like;" and immediately turned round and walked into the after cabin. The words "Port the helm!" were scarcely uttered, when Sir Charles ordered me down with directions to commence firing on the larboard side. On my return to the quarter-deck, I found the Formidable passing between two French ships, each nearly touching us. We were followed by the Namur, and the rest of the ships astern; and from that moment the victory was decided in our favour. You may naturally suppose I was very young at the time; but the circumstances made such an impression on my mind, that they are as fresh in my memory as if it occurred but yesterday; and I much doubt if there is a man now living who saw and heard so much of the transaction as myself, except, probably, my friend Sir Joseph Yorke, who was also a brother aide-de-camp. Having thus stated mere matters of fact just as they occurred, and within my own knowledge, I leave any man to draw what inference he pleases; hut I would ask him, supposing the Admiral had had such a conversation, either jointly or separately with Mr. Clerk, previous to their leaving England, or that these great and gallant officers had ever consulted together on the subject of breaking the enemy's line, would such a difference of opinion have existed, or such a kind of controversy, as I have related, have taken place? I say, no. I am most clearly convinced, and my mind most thoroughly satisfied, that the idea of breaking the line never entered into the imagination of even your gallant Father, till the moment of his leaning on the hammocks, and looking towards the enemy's ships. His deep thought at that instant-his sudden raising his head from his hand, as if he had just then settled something in his mind-the quick way of his turning round, and the anxious look he gave when he said, "Dash, where's Sir George?"-all convince me that the idea of breaking the line first entered his mind at that moment, and that he seized it with avidity. I think I have sufficiently shown, to the satisfaction of every impartial man, the great probability, if not absolute certainty, that the idea rose in the mind of your excellent Father at the very time I have pointed out; and that this great event decided the battle is beyond doubt. This is my firm opinion; I have held it for seven and forty years, and I shall continue in the same sentiments to the last moment of my existence. I had the good fortune to be much noticed by the Captain of the Fleet, daily and hourly in his cabin, and my time was much occupied in copying various documents; amongst them was a "Comparative Statement of the Force of the French and English Fleets, showing the Weight of Metal and Shot thrown in a Broadside from each." If, peradventure, you could find such a document amongst your Father's papers, I shall be thankful for a copy. I am sure I wrote some hundreds, and kept one myself, but it has disappeared in the lapse of time.

I shall feel great satisfaction in giving the son of so good and so great a man any further information in my power. I have the honour to be,

With great esteem, Your very obliged and devoted humble servant, Ca. DASHWOOD, Capt. R.N.

Copy of a Letter from Captain Sir Charles Dashwood, K.C.B., to the Editor of the United Service Journal.

Torquay, Devon,
January 30, 1830.

MR. EDITOR,

I have just seen in the last Quarterly Review, a very long statement on the subject of Lord Rodney's battle on the 12th of April, 1782, in reply to the one published by Sir Howard Douglas, and in which my letter to that officer is canvassed with no small degree of acrimony. I am not so weak as to enter the list of controversy with such fearful adversaries, yet it is necessary I should give some explanation in my own defence; and though they may turn, and twist, and criticise all and every expression contained in that letter, it does not alter the case one iota; and whatever ridicule they may endeavour to cast on what they have been facetiously pleased to term the "C wheel-scene," the whole is, nevertheless, substantially true, and with all their ingenuity they cannot confute it;-they must at least do me the justice to believe that I could not have been actuated by interested motives when I tell them that to this hour I have not the honour of even a personal acquaintance with Sir Howard Douglas; nor did I know he was a son of the late Captain of the Fleet until about six months ago, when he wrote, requesting I would give him such information on breaking the enemy's line as came within my own knowledge. I did so without reserve, and I can assure you, Mr. Editor, it is a matter of no importance to me whether the merit of that great deed is fixed on the escutcheon of Lord Rodney, or on that of Sir Charles Douglas; but called upon by the son of the latter, a perfect stranger, I conscientiously imparted what I heard and saw. Beyond this, I have nothing more to say than to regret that such a delicate question should ever have been brought before the public, and to assure the friends of my Lord Rodney that it never was my intention to show the slightest disrespect to the memory of so great and so distinguished an officer. I cannot, therefore, but be much distressed that it should even be supposed that when I mentioned the Admiral's going into the after-cabin, it could be construed into his going off the deck; every naval officer is aware, though the Reviewers may not be, that the cabin is merely a continuation of the quarter-deck. It is certain the Admiral was in the stern and quarter-galleries the greater part of the battle, and it was in the latter situation, whilst leaning out of the window, viewing his own and the enemy's fleet, that I presented him with a glass of lemonade which he had desired me to make. I never said that the Admiral was not on the quarter-deck at the moment the Formidable was passing through the enemy's line, for he was repeatedly in and out, but merely observed that when he sanctioned that operation, he turned to the cabin; but how far he advanced, or how long he remained, is impossible for me to say, as at that moment I was ordered below to give the necessary directions for opening the fire on the larboard side. The whole of my observations do not, in point of time, occupy more than five or six minutes, commencing whilst the Captain of the Fleet was leaning on the hammocks, meditating, as I still think, on some great design, to the conclusion of the "wheel-scene," and as it would not take up more than from ten to fifteen seconds to go from the wheel to the stern gallery, and about twenty more from thence to the gangway, it is both easy and clear the Chief was on that very spot at the critical moment of passing under the stern of the Glorieux, as stated by Sir Gilbert Blane, and then it was, I take for granted, the Admiral desired him (both the aides-de-camp being previously dispatched) to go down and order the guns to be depressed;-I do, therefore, most cordially join with, and beg to corroborate, the statement of the Reviewers, "that the Chief was on the quarter-deck, before, during, and after the Formidable passed through the enemy's line." No one ever asserted to the contrary, or doubted it: then how they can, even by possibility, construe this into the Admiral's retirement into the cabin, is best known to themselves. But it is neither candid nor just thus to torture my meaning to the dishonour and prejudice of so great a man. I disclaim it with indignation. However, young as I certainly was when this great battle was fought, yet early impressions are the most lasting, particularly one of such an interesting nature as those described; but if they imagine it has lain dormant in my breast for seven and forty years, and only now brought forward for the first time, merely at the instigation of Sir Howard Douglas, or any other man, they are much mistaken; for I have mentioned it in all societies whenever it has been the subject of conversation during the whole of that long period.

I have the honour to be, Mr. Editor,
Your most obedient humble servant,
CHARLES DASHWOOD, Captain, Royal Navy.

Letter from Vice-Admiral the Hon. Sir Joseph Sydney Yorke, K.C.B. , who served in the Formidable in the Battle of the 12th of April.

"About six o'clock on the morning of the 12th of April, 1782, Sir Charles went into Lord Rodney's cabin, who was then a-bed, and told him that Providence had given him the French fleet on his lee-bow, on which the Admiral got up, and gave his general orders to prepare for battle. At half-past seven the engagement began. At eleven A. M. there appeared an opening sufficient for our ships to divide the French line. Sir Charles observed to the Admiral, that there was now a fine opportunity for severing the rear and half the centre from the Ville-de-Paris; to which Lord Rodney replied, that it was a very hazardous experiment. Sir Charles said, the more danger the more glory, if it succeeded, which he doubted not it would. But the Admiral still objected, and called out to the helm, (for we were then, as the wind favoured us, luffing up,) No nearer! A discussion, which it is unnecessary to repeat, then took place between the Admiral and his First Captain, in which "Sir Charles maintained his opinion, and again called out to the helm 'to luff.' " Upon further consideration, Sir George Rodney determined, most gallantly, with true greatness of mind, to adopt the advice of the Captain of the Fleet; and the writer adds "The Formidable then pushed through the line, amidst the shouts and applauses of our fleet, and by this gallant manoeuvre fied the fortune of the day."

The gallant officer by whom the letter and narrative, of which the preceding are extracts, were written, had confidential access to the cabins of both those officers, and knew perfectly well all that was going on; and he has assured me [Sir Howard] that there was positively "no premeditated plan of breaking the line entertained."

Letter from Charles Thesiger, Esq. (Copy.)

13, St. Alban's Place,
St. James's Square,
17th Feb. 1830.

Sir,-I have just seen a recent number of the Quarterly Review, containing a laboured article, endeavouring by specious argument to invalidate the facts you had adduced in support of the claim which you had so meritoriously asserted in favour of your lamented Father, as having been chiefly instrumental to the victory gained on the 12th April, 1782, by the daring exploit of carrying the British fleet through the French line; and knowing that I had in my possession a letter from my brother, the late Sir Frederick Thesiger, who acted as aide-de-camp to Lord Rodney on that important day, I have referred to it, and hope you will not consider me intrusive in having forwarded some extracts relating to the action, as strongly corroborative of the claim you have endeavoured to establish, and coinciding in a remarkable manner with the living testimonies which you have already been enabled to procure. My brother, at the time of the action, was twenty-four years of age, and was well known in the navy at the time of his death, when he had attained the rank of post-captain. He accompanied Lord Nelson to Copenhagen, where he also acted as his aide-de-camp, and was charged by his Lordship with his letter to the Crown Prince, which caused a cessation of hostilities. His life is to be found in the Naval Chronicle, very minutely and correctly given; and he was not only a gallant officer, but a man of unquestionable veracity.

I have the honour to be, &c.
(Signed) CHARLES THESIGER.

To Sir Howard Douglas. If you should have the least curiosity to compare the original with those parts which I have copied, I shall at all times be ready to produce my brother's letter.

Extracts from Frederick Thesiger's Letters, commenced December, 1782, and continued till 25th of February, 1783.

He had before announced his safety, and the event of the battle of the 12th of April, and this was in answer to one of mine, desiring to be furnished with more particular information. C. T. "About seven on Sunday morning, being the 8th, our cruizers made the signal for the enemy being under sail. We immediately made the signal for our ships to get under way; and in the evening, about nine o'clock, one of our ships hailed us, and informed us the French were close a-head of us. We kept on our course until we could plainly discern their lights, and then made the signal for the fleet to lay-to, being in the order of sailing. The Admiral called for his aides-de-camp on the 9th, before we began to engage, and finding they were mere boys, he told Captain Symonds to let him have somebody he could depend upon; he immediately introduced me, who was his aide-decamp, and the Admiral was satisfied." The action of the 9th of April is then described, which was only partial, sixteen or seventeen of our ships being mere spectators, having no wind to manage them. "The ship astern of us came into action; the rest of the centre and all the rear were prevented, from the cause 1 have mentioned: we lost three men and about ten wounded. Lieutenant Hale was among the killed-a very amiable young man." The cause which led to the action on the 12th of April is then explained. "We certainly sailed much superior to the enemy, our ships being all coppered, whereas the French had not twenty clean ships. The superiority of our sailing was very conspicuous, for although the French fleet had got off so great a distance to windward, yet before night we came up within three or four miles of them, and had we carried the same sail, we should have brought them to action long before; we may consider the accident which happened to the Zele, as a very favourable circumstance to us. She got foul of the Ville de-Paris in the night and carried away her foremast and bowsprit, which brought the fleet very much to leeward; in the morning of the 12th we saw the Zele in tow by a frigate, which was going with her into Guadaloupe. We sent two or three ships after her, but the French fleet bearing down, we recalled them, and they formed themselves into the line of battle close to the wind: the enemy did the same, but they were too late, for they thought to pass our line at the distance they did on the 9th, and in every action this war; but they fairly entrapped themselves, and we chose our distance. The van and the centre divisions a-head of us,passed close along the French line. The Formidable went through, and the rest of the centre and rear divisions followed. * neither should we have got through if his orders had been obeyed. * Sir Charles Douglas is the man who had the sole merit of fighting the Formidable; * * * * * * * * * * * * * As we were passing the French line, it was glorious and animating to hear Sir Charles giving his orders with so much clearness, and at the same time so much elated; it had a wonderful effect upon me, and I felt myself honoured fighting by a person possessing so much magnanimity. He conducted the Formidable as close along the French line as it was possible; the five or six last ships I could have thrown cold shot aboard them, they were so near. The Admiral cried, 'No nearer;' Sir Charles, ' Luff, my boys, and the day's our own.' No nearer, I say,' repeated the Admiral. 'Don't fall off,' answered Sir Charles. The Admiral came to me, and ordered me to go to the wheel and see the helm put up; but as Sir Charles kept incessantly crying, 'Luff, my boys, luff,' and it is always an inferior officer's duty to obey the last command, therefore I did not put the Admiral's orders into execution." "The letter so often adverted to, and to which you attach some importance, contains matter of a private and domestic nature, which prevents me from trusting it out of my own possession; but those parts relating to the naval events of that period may be inspected by any one on either side of the question.

(Signed) C. T."

Extract of a Letter from Frederick Knight, Esq., now living at Stonehouse, Devon, who was Sir Charles Douglas's Secretary at the time of the action, was present on the quarter-deck, and whose peculiar duty it was to observe and note all that passed.

Union Street, Stonehouse,
February 26th, 1830.

"In reply to your inquiries concerning the subject of breaking the enemy's line on the 12th of April, 1782, I beg to state, that the merit attached to that bold and fortunate manoeuvre rests wholly on the late Sir Charles Douglas. Sir Charles saw an opening at the stern of the Ville-de-Paris, and, on meeting Lord Rodney, said, 'I give you joy of the victory; only break the enemy's line, and we shall have possession of the Ville-de-Paris before night.' "-The writer then goes on to state, that at first the Admiral objected, and in very strong terms. "But Sir Charles persisted in the propriety of breaking the line, and said, 'Mr. Harris, put the helm a-port.' The Admiral ordered it a-starboard. The Admiral then went into the cabin. He remained a very short time, and then returned to the quarter-deck again, when Sir Charles repeated his desire to break the line, when the Admiral said, ' Do as you please. The helm was then put to port, and the Formidable passed through the line, and was followed by the Namur and the other British ships in gallant style. The enemy were put into the greatest confusion, and were terror-struck by this new manner of fighting. "From the situation I held at the time (Secretary to Sir C. Douglas), I think I may positively assert that the idea of breaking the line was never mentioned between him and the Admiral till the time of its being put into execution, and from what I have already stated, the thought was momentary, and originated with Sir Charles.

(Signed) FREDERICK KNIGHT."

Extract of a Letter from Captain Blaney, who was a Midshipman on board the Formidable in the Action.

Plymouth, February 3d, 1830.

"MY DEAR SIR,-I am favoured with your letter of the 1st instant, and hasten to comply with your wishes. "I do not think there was the smallest intention of breaking the enemy's line, until a few minutes before the opportunity presented itself of doing so with the effect that followed. There can be no doubt of an altercation between the Commander-in-Chief and the Captain of the Fleet, whether the helm should be put a-starboard or port, which was alternately done, and even a-port by the motion of Sir Charles's hand. In this situation was the Formidable, making an angle with the ship our second a head, when the helm was desired to be put a-port without further opposition. Sir Charles had frequently called to the man at the wheel, 'Luff, my man, luff; keep her close at it. Almost in an instant were four of the enemy's ships opposed to our larboard broadside, who had, on our breaking through, fallen aboard each other. "It was generally understood that Lord Rodney said, 'do as you please, Sir Charles,' and from this permission the helm was ordered down, that is a-port. The Admiral was mostly in his chair on the quarter-deck, and with difficulty could walk with the gout. My journal for the Formidable from December, 1781, to April, 1783, is at this moment before me: the transactions of the 9th and 12th April were wrote the next day." Should you have any wish to peruse them, you have only to say the word.

Believe me, my dear Sir,

With much esteem, your's very truly,

G. W. BLANEY."

Extract of a Letter from Sir G. Blane.

"My being late in coming home when I received your letter, prevented me from answering it so soon as you wished. "I can have no objection to your inserting the note you propose. I certainly never heard either the name of Mr. Clerk, or his work, till some time after the peace, when in England." The Admiral certainly was a good deal in the cabin under the poop during part of the action, and I employed myself in assisting to work a nine-pounder there. But a short time before the breaking of the line, we were both on the quarter-deck, as must have been the case, when on observing us fast approaching the Glorieux, he looked round, and seeing none of his aides-de-camp, he sent me to the lower gun-deck to order them to lower their metal. I think it likely that it was while I was so engaged, that what Sir Charles Dashwood told you took place. I should like much that Sir C. Dashwood were to see my printed account of the action; and as I do not mention the circumstance of my being sent to the lower gun-deck, could you ask him whether he remembers it? I abstained from publishing it, as it would look vainglorious and out of character for me. There is not the smallest item of contradiction or inconsistency between my printed account and the statement you showed me.

(Signed) GILBERT BLANE."

"It is not much out of place here to remark, that it was considered as a fortunate circumstance for the service that the Commander-in-Chief of the fleet in the West Indies, in the memorable campaign of 1782, should have had about his person to assist and advise him, so able an officer as Sir Charles Douglas, he himself being almost always in such bad health, either from illness or convalescence from the gout, from debility and unequal spirits, as to render him less equal to the fatiguing and anxious duties inseparable from such high responsibility."

- *Memoir on Military Punishment*, by Sir Gilbert Blane.

Extract of a Letter from Frederick Edgecombe, Esq. Victualling Office, February 5th, 1830.

"Immediately after parting with you the other day, I committed to paper the impression on my mind of the transaction in question. It is as follows: "When opposite the Glorieux, Sir C. Douglas is reported to have said, 'Now is the glorious moment for breaking the enemy's line;' Lord Rodney to have replied, 'Suppose the fleet should be scattered;' Sir Charles to have rejoined,' The fleet will not be scattered;'-that port and starboard was alternately ordered by those officers; that in the end Lord Rodney said, 'Do as you please,' and went into his cabin, when Sir Charles said, 'Down with the helm? Of course there were many versions of this conversation in circula tion, but I have the strongest recollection I have stated the substance of what I heard on joining the Formidable, in July 1782.

(Signed) F. EDGECOMBE."

Extract of a Letter from Lieutenant Cleiland, of the Fame, 74, who was present in the Action, to Sir Charles Douglas, dated Fame, Monday morning.

Fame, Monday Noon.

"SIR CHARLES,-I have been exceedingly unhappy in hearing of your indisposition, and more so by not having it in my power to have called in person. "I pray to God, Sir Charles, for your health; which is of more consequence to the nation, than two-thirds of the nation are at present acquainted with. I have wrote as far as my humble abilities can scan over the ever memorable day, and this I'm sure, that Royalty, if not Majesty, will see. And it contains nothing but truth,-it will add lustre to those who gloriously fought and pointed out so masterly a stroke that records cannot show.

I have the honour, &c. &c.
(Signed) ROBT. CLEILAND."

Extract of a Letter from the late General Edward Smith, to Sir Charles Douglas, dated Charles Street, December, 13th, 1782.

"Hughes in the East Indies has had hard blows, and has fought well; but I think if manoeuvre was more fashionable, and Sir Charles Douglas's system with De Grasse closely copied and imitated, we should save lives and gain more glory, perhaps not so complete as yours, but still sufficient to master always the enemy we may have to deal with."

Letter from Captain Rotherham, Lieutenant of the Monarch, Collingwood's Captain in the Battle of Trafalgar.

Royal Hospital, Greenwich,
November 7th, 1829. "

DEAR SIR,-I beg you will accept my sincere thanks for the honour done me by your having forwarded your excellent pamphlet, containing the important facts relative to the glorious victory obtained by our fleet on the 12th April, 1782. "Being myself a lieutenant of H. M. S. Monarch, on that occasion, I have it in my power, by a reference to the plans and minutes I then made, to vouch for the truth and justness of your statement, being always of opinion that the success of that eventful day may be attributed to that masterly (but before unheard-of) manoeuvre of passing through the enemy's line, and which, from conversations I have had with a distinguished officer in that fleet, now defunct, and who was Sir George Rodney's second astern, I am as fully convinced as man can be, that the invention originated with your zealous and revered Father, whose memory deserves to be retained in grateful remembrance by the service, to which he was an ornament, and our beloved country, which was benefited so materially by his able exertions.

I have the honour to be, &c. &c.
(Signed) EDWARD ROTHERHAM."

Extract of a Letter, dated Stoke, Devonport, 6th February, 1830, from Captain Sayer, Royal Navy, to F. Edgecombe, Esq.

"I was myself in the battle as a midshipman on board the Anson, Captain Blair, (who was killed in the early part of it), and was myself slightly wounded in the leg: our lieutenants were--st, Anthony Gibbs; 2d, James May, and 3d, Sir J. Athol Wood, all since dead; and I remember perfectly the opinion was, on approaching the enemy's fleet, Sir Charles Douglas signified the fine opportunity now coming for going through the line, which Lord Rodney was supposed to be much against, fearing it would cause great confusion among our own ships, and probably separate them; however, it was said, that Sir Charles being so firmly decided on making the attempt, that his lordship was induced to give it up to him to act as he pleased; and in consequence, the Formidable was kept to the wind by order of Sir Charles, and the enemy's line was broken through: of course I was too young to know much about the matter, but I have always understood that the line would not have been broken but for the firmness of Sir Charles Douglas.

(Signed) GEORGE SAYER."

Letter from Sir David Milne.

Coldstream, 18th February, 1830.

"Sir,-I had the honour yesterday of receiving your letter of the 13th instant. In answer to which I can only state what was generally the opinion in the fleet regarding the breaking of the French, on the 12th of April, 1782. " It was generally understood, that at the time the centre of our fleet came along the French line engaging as they passed, that at that moment a difference of opinion prevailed between the Commander-in-Chief, Sir George B. Rodney and Sir Charles Douglas, Captain of the Fleet, regarding passing through the French line; that this was not settled until the event actually took place. The Commander-in-Chief, not approving of the measure, was calling to the man at the wheel to starboard the helm, while Sir Charles Douglas, who was for the measure, was calling out to port the helm; and during this altercation the Formidable passed through the line, followed by the ships astern, thus throwing that division of the French fleet between two fires. I was at that time in the Canada, commanded by the Hon. Captain Cornwallis, the third ship astern of the Formidable. This is, as far as was generally understood at the time, what occurred regarding the above-mentioned manoeuvre, and I have never understood it otherwise; this was also corroborated by an old and intimate acquaintance of mine, now dead, a Mr. Norris, afterwards lieutenant Norris, who was on board the Formidable at the time, and, I believe, on the quarter-deck, who often mentioned the circumstances to me. "This is what occurs to my recollection respecting your queries, and the impression at the time was, and always has been, as I have stated above.

I have the honour to be, &c. &c. (Signed) DAVID MILNE."

Letter from Admiral Lawford of the Namur.

MY DEAR SIR ALEXANDER,-Should you see Sir Howard Douglas, will you have the goodness to thank him for the honour, I conceive, he does me, in sending me his Statement of Facts respecting the Breaking of the Enemy's Line in the Action of the 12th of April, 1782. " I have read it with much interest, as it recalls to my recollection all the circumstances of that important event. It was my good fortune to be a Lieutenant in the Namur, the ship immediately astern of the Formidable, and remember it was generally said, and believed, that Sir Charles Douglas had the merit of pointing out to the Commander-in-Chief the glorious opportunity which then presented itself of passing through the opening in the enemy's line. " With best compliments to Lady Bryce, in which Mrs. Lawford begs to unite.

I remain, my dear Sir, &c. &c. (Signed) JOHN LAWFORD."

Letter from Captain Tobin of the Namur.

Teignmouth, February 9th, 1830.

" It is somewhat strange that I never knew any thing of a third edition of Mr. Clerke's Naval Tactics; nor can I now find any account of it in the periodical journals; but, whatever may be stated in the work, respecting the breaking of the line on the 12th of April, my mind has always been under an impression that it was put in force on a sudden suggestion of your excellent Father to the Commander-in-Chief, and the strong testimony recently adduced in your pamphlet, cannot but (of course) serve to give stability to such an opinion. Indeed, what right have I to doubt, when two officers, of high reputation and integrity, who were on the quarter-deck of the Formidable, and whose duty it was to watch every word, look, and motion of the Commanderin-Chief and Captain of the Fleet, declare such to have been the case?

(Signed) GEO. TOBIN."

Copy of a Letter from Admiral R. Dacres. First Lieutenant of the Alcide.

Bathford, February 27th, 1830. " Sir,-In replying to your letter of the 20th instant, I beg to state that I cannot, after such a lapse of time, presume to give a positive opinion on the question you put to me. On the 12th of April, 1782, I was first lieutenant of the Alcide, the third ship in the van, therefore know little of what happened in the rear, but perfectly remember, on the smoke clearing up, seeing the Formidable and Namur to windward of both lines. The impression on my mind was then, and ever has been, that the breaking the line was accidental, and never contemplated;- had it been so, the fleet ought to have known it. There, no doubt, were reports in the fleet that your Father was the person who suggested it to Sir George.

I have the honour to be, &c. &c.

(Signed) RICH. DACRES."

Extract of a Letter from Sir Arthur Legge, Prince George.

Blackheath, 27th January, 1830.

" In the action of the 12th of April, I served as midshipman on board the Prince George, and was quarterd on the main-deck; we were second to Sir Francis Drake in the van; I could not, therefore, see what passed in the centre, but I perfectly recollect that it was reported among the officers of the fleet when we got to Port Royal, and generally believed, that the cutting through the enemy's line was suggested to Sir George Rodney by Sir Charles Douglas, Captain of the Fleet, though I can't say that I heard Sir George had objected to the measure.

Believe me, &c. &c.

(Signed) A. K. LEGGE."

Copy of a Letter from Lieutenant Frederick Maitland, in Garrison at Port Royal.

London, 28th January, 1830.

"I send you in writing the substance of what I expressed to you a few days ago, when I happened to converse with you on the subject now debated, relative to Admiral Lord Rodney and Sir Charles Douglas. " That I was in Jamaica, being then an officer in the 14th Regiment, when our fleet and the French captured ships arrived at Port Royal; that, at that time, the action which had just taken place was the common subject of conversation; and that it was very generally said and understood, that the manoeuvre which had decided the victory, meaning the breaking the enemy's line, originated with Sir Charles Douglas, and that it was Sir Charles who proposed to and urged the measure with the Admiral. " This I heard certainly then in general conversations, and I have often since heard the same opinion expressed among naval officers.

(Signed) FRED. MAITLAND."

Letter from Captain Fyffe. London.

Albany Street, Edinburgh,
19th February, 1830.

"Sir,-I was favoured with your's some days since, but delayed replying to it till I could see some brother officers (here) that I knew had been in the action of the 12th of April, 1782. I was not in that fleet with Sir George Rodney, but was in the London, at Jamaica, when the squadron came down with the prizes, and the impression is strong on my memory that the prevailing opinion amongst the officers was that Sir Charles Douglas had the merit of planning and carrying into effect the breaking of the French line of battle on that day. Captain Alexander Robert Kerr (residing here), who was midshipman of the Endymion repeating frigate on that day, has the same opinion as to the officers. Captain Spear says, in his note to me, ' I was midshipman in the Marlborough, in the action of the 12th of April, 1782, but quartered on the lower-deck, therefore can only speak from hearsay; that ship led the line on that day and fetched upon opposite tack to the enemy, within five or six ships of their van ship, then edged away along their line; recollects it was afterwards said that the breaking of the line was accidental, but had been suggested by Sir Charles Douglas to Sir George Rodney, and that Clerke's Naval Tactics had nothing do with it.' I am sorry that I cannot give you better information on a subject that you appear much interested in.

(Signed) JOHN FYFFE."

Letter from Dr. Black.

"Kirkaldy, March 15th, 1830. " Sir,-I had the honour to receive your letter of the 8th instant, in which you request to know what I recollect concerning the opinion in the fleet formed of the memorable engagement of the 12th of April, 1782. " I was in the West Indies at the time, but not present at that brilliant achievement. The ship I belonged to was at Jamaica, where the victorious fleet with the captured ships came to, immediately after the engagement, and I had considerable intercourse with the officers of many of the ships. The facts generally stated were, that Sir Charles Douglas noticed the practicability of breaking the French line, and pointed it out to Lord Rodney, and urged the measure strenuously. I do not recollect hearing that Lord Rodney had premeditated or predetermined on this mode of attack whenever the fleets should meet. " It is now near fifty years since, and I am fourscore years of age; yet I think my recollections are distinct still concerning the share of merit which was allowed Sir Charles Douglas, by those who were present, and knew all the circumstances of that eventful day.

I have the honour to be, &c.
(Signed) W. BLACK."

APPENDIX G

INFORMATION REGARDING SIR CHARLES DOUGLAS' VALET, GEORGE STEWART, WHO WAS WITH HIM ABOARD THE FORMIDABLE ON 12 APRIL 1782

(Reprinted from *Naval Evolutions* by Sir Howard Douglas)

The Surveyor General of Upper Canada, Mr. Hurd, had occasion to remain for a few days at Utica in the United States, on his way from New Brunswick, in which Province he had held the like situation, to York. During his stay at Utica, he was waited upon by an aged person, who stated, that having been many years in the service of the late Sir Charles Douglas, and hearing that Mr. Hurd had recently been in New Brunswick, he, the applicant, (George Stewart,) wished to make enquiry respecting his old master's son, (Sir Howard,) who had been Governor of that province. Mr. Hurd received the applicant, and finding by documents which he produced, that he had long attended my Father in the capacity of Valet, and that he was on board the Formidable, in the battle; he, Mr. Hurd, questioned him very closely as to all the particulars which passed under his own eye, in relation to my Father.

The man detailed all the occurrences of the day, clearly and distinctly, and explained, that he had the best opportunity of seeing and hearing what passed, by being immediately about my Father's person, as his valet, before the action commenced, and by being posted to one of the quarter-deck guns during the battle, that he might be in the way to attend upon his master, if needful.

Finding the account given by Stewart to corroborate remarkably what Sir Charles Dashwood and others affirm, as to the facts of the case, Mr. Hurd told the faithful old man, that the splendid service performed on that occasion by his late master, had been much disputed and obscured, and that if he, Stewart, was clear and positive as to the truth of his averment, that his deposition to that effect would no doubt be acceptable to the members of the family. The man immediately expressed the strongest and most affectionate desire to depose to the truth of what he stated, and this was accordingly done, in due form, in presence of Tho. Rockwell, Esq., Notary Public, at Utica, on the 19th of March, 1832. I well remember the person named George Stewart-Black George; but to put beyond all doubt the fact, that the deponent was my Father's valet, in 1782, I annex certified extracts from the documents in his possession; and having referred to Sir Gilbert Blane as to the circumstance of George Stewart having been stationed to a gun on the quarter-deck, received an answer, of which the following is an extract.

" June 9th, 1832.-I have great pleasure in certifying that George Stewart is no impostor. He was, and no doubt is now, (but I had no idea of his being in existence) a little, round, squat African, much attached to Sir Charles, and I have often heard Sir Charles express himself with great partiality towards him, as an honest and faithful servant."

Further, Sir Gilbert states, that he perfectly recollects George Stewart assisted in fighting the quarter-deck gun at which Sir Gilbert stationed himself.

Copies of Certificates of Servitude and Character exhibited by George Stewart, the late Admiral Sir Charles Douglas's Servant, to Mr. S. P. Hurd, late Surveyor-General of New Brunswick, and now of Upper Canada, and Dr. William Turner, M. D. an English Physician, and compared with the Originals in the presence of the Gentlemen of Utica, State of New York, whose Declaration is hereunto attached,

"I herewith certify that the statement drawn up by Mr. S. P. Hurd, late Surveyor-General of New Brunswick, and now of Upper Canada, is in every particular perfectly correct; that I was present during the examination referred to; that I afterwards asked the said George Stewart a variety of questions, most especially as to the conversation on board the Formidable between Sir George

Rodney and Sir Charles Douglas, but found it impossible to stagger his evidence on any one point whatsoever."

I also declare that the accompanying Certificates of servitude and character are faithful copies of the originals. WM. TURNER, M.D."

Utica, State of New York,
March 19, 1832.

"United States of America, State of New York. " On the 19th March, 1832, before me came the within-named William Turner, who, being by me duly sworn, made oath to the truth of the within Certificate. " In testimony whereof I have hereunto set my name, and affixed my official seal, the day and year above written.

L. S. THOMAS ROCKWELL,
Notary Public." " Copy."

No. I.-Sir Charles Douglas. "These are to certify, whomsoever it may concern, that George Stewart, a native of the Island of Barbados, and a free man, served me as my valet de chambre on board his Majesty's ships Duke, Formidable, and Resistance, and on shore as occasion required, from the beginning of the month of May, 1779, to the date hereof, during all which time he ever behaved himself with diligence, sobriety, honesty, fidelity, and respect towards me, and I hereby recommend him as a person deserving of having confidence reposed in him accordingly. He is of a good capacity, having taught himself to read, write, and tolerably well to cast accompts, and is discharged from my service at his own request. " Given under my hand on board His Majesty's ship Hermione, in Halifax harbour, this first day of August, 1785.

(Signed) CHA. DOUGLAS."

No. II.- W. Bentinck, Esq. "This is to certify, that George Stewart lived with me six months, during which time he behaved himself with diligence, sobriety, and honesty.

(Signed) W. BENTINCK.
Halifax, Nova Scotia,
March 9, 1786."

No. III.-Lady Douglas. " George Stewart lived with the late Sir Charles Douglas near ten years, during which time he behaved with remarkable diligence and attention, was an affectionate, honest, and trusty servant. " Witness my hand, London, March 21, 1789.

(Signed) JANE DOUGLAS."

No. IV.-Captain David Knox, R.N. "The bearer hereof, George Stewart, was in the service of Sir Charles Douglas, Bart. during the space of ten years, and he has since served with me for the space of two years more, until he was discharged by his own desire to reside in New York, during which time he served with great reputation as an honest, sober, and attentive man. As witness my hand, this 4th day of August, at New York, 1791.

(Signed) DAVID KNOX,
Captain in the British Navy.

No. V.-Jonas Platt, Judge. " I certify that the bearer, George Stewart, a black man, has resided in this town several years, and has uniformly maintained the character of a sober, industrious, and honest man, and as such I recommend him wherever he may go.

(Signed) JONAS PLATT."
Utica, 12th October, 1824."

No. VI.-Rev. H. Anthon. "This is to certify that George Stewart is a Communicant of the Parish of Trinity Church, Utica, and that during my acquaintance with him I have noticed nothing inconsistent with his obligations as such. (Signed) HENRY ANTHON, late Rector of Trinity Church, Utica." " Utica, State of New York, U. S. April 25, 1829." " United States of America, State of New York. " J. H. Rathbone, Counsellor at Law, residing in the city of Utica, State aforesaid, being duly affirmed, says, that he has for many years been intimately acquainted with the Honourable Jonas Platt, late Justice of the Supreme Court of the State of New York, and with the Rev. Henry Anthon of the city of New York, late Rector of Trinity Church, Utica, that he has examined the original Certificates, of which the above (Nos. 5 and 6) are copies, and knows them to be in the proper handwriting of the gentlemen whose names are subscribed thereto: and further, that he has compared the above copies of Certificates, Nos. 1, 2, 3, and 4, with the originals, and that they are true copies.

J. H. RATHBONE." "United States of America, State of New York. S " On the 20th March, 1832, before me came J. H. Rathbone, to me known to be the same person described in, and who subscribed the above affidavit, and affirmed to the truth thereof. " In testimony whereof I have hereunto affixed my official seal, and subscribed my name thereto, this same day and year above written.

THOMAS ROCKWELL,
Notary Public." (L. S.)

Copy of a Letter from John Barrow, Esq. Secretary to the Admiralty, to Commodore Barrie, C.B. touching the Claims of George Stewart to a Pension.

"Admiralty Office, 19th November, 1829. " SIR, (Having laid before my Lords Commissioners of the Admiralty your letter of the 17th September last, in behalf of George Stewart, whose services and destitute situation you have recommended to their Lordships favourable consideration, I am commanded to acquaint you, that it appears that the said man served only six years and three months [1]in the Royal Navy, from which he was discharged in the year 1785, then only twenty-six years of age, and that under these circumstances their Lordships have no means of affording him any assistance.

I am, Sir, Your most obedient humble servant,

(Signed) JOHN BARROW."

---

[1] See the annexed Memorandum touching this. Memorandum. 'The six years and three months seem to be made out thus:-from May 1779, when the said Stewart joined Sir Charles Douglas and his discharge by Sir Charles in August 1785. He, however, states that he was again borne on the Adamant's books after Sir Charles Douglas's death, when he accompanied Captain D. Knox. See his certificate. This point may increase the claim for servitude, and should be inquired into. S. P. HURD."

APPENDIX D

EXCERPT FROM A LETTER FROM SIR CHARLES DOUGLAS TO HIS SISTER, HELENA BAILLIE, REGARDING THE NEWS THAT THE IDEA OF BREAKING THE LINE HAD ORIGINATED WITH JOHN CLERK OF ELDIN (1783)

Mrs. Baillie Olive Bank Near Edinburgh
Formidable at St. Lucia March ye 2d 1783

...the matter in Question too ridiculous and groundless to be seriously treated, for as much as I am mentioned or alluded to therein Deserve to be treated, as a product of Arrogance and Impertinence towards me and my being mentioned therein at all, in the way you say, is highly injurious to him who commanded in chief on that celebrated Day, who certainly did not stand in need of any such instructions derived from Lt. Clark...

...It is he, commanding a Fleet or Army in whose mind the ideas rise with the occasion and who seizes the decisive moment when it presents itself that gains a decisive Victory, not the dull man who simply acts from the instructions of others, no matter how respectable.

APPENDIX E

LETTER FROM SIR CHARLES DOUGLAS TO HIS SISTER, HELENA BAILLIE, REGARDING HIS LAST TRIP TO SCOTLAND AND HIS RIFT WITH HIS DAUGHTER (1789)

To Mrs Baillie at Olive Bank Near Edinburgh
Written in great Haste! God save the King!

Yours Dear Sister of the 16th is, to my unspeakable pleasure! this morning came to hand. And I shall now struggle hard, to get thro' what I have to do, as fast as possible, that I may be enabled, with propriety, to undertake my long-proposed Journey to Scotland, which, as my time there will be but short at best, and as Lady Douglas has caught a fresh and a severe cold; or; more properly speaking; has relapsed into her former one; I shall perofrm at last alone. You need not therefore, take the trouble of addressing me here, as I hope for the pleasure of seeing you soon. I shall not in that case have occasion; according to the purport of my letters of yesterday both to you and him; to trouble Mr. Sandilands (I pray you write so to him on the receipt hereof) to conduct my two Boys to London, but shall have that pleasure myself if I should persevere in my resolution, of having them brought South: as being of the Opinion, that it is now time, to adopt some new plan of education for them. I think they'd both acquire good French and Dutch were they sent into Brabant, before they can be received into the Royal Academy at Norwich—Or, what perhaps might do as well, they'd both learn good French; in Canada; long before the Expiration of my North American command: but more of this hereafter. In the meantime, I promise, that no late disagreeable things are to be so much as spoken of! And that nobody is so much as to make mention to me anything of my undutiful eldest Daughter! The

King be well forever and forever! From the parent stock of Your most affectionate Bro. & Faithful Friend.

Ch.s Douglas

P:S: I beg to be remembered to Mr Baillie, Mr Smith, Mr Ross and Mrs Ross. My eldest daughter did not deserve the confidences which you and I reposed in her. The House of Peers adjourns until Thursday because the King is better

APPENDIX F

SIR CHARLES DOUGLAS' TESTIMONY AT THE COURT MARTIAL OF ADMIRAL AUGUSTUS KEPPEL

(From *The Trial of the Honourable Augustus Keppel, Admiral of the Blue Squadron*)

Sir CHARLES DOUGLAS of the Stirling Castle, called and sworn.

Admiral Keppel: Did the French fleet shew any intention of coming to action, from the time they were discovered to the 27th, when they were brought to battle?

A. By no means; to the best of my knowledge, they ever did endeavour to avoid it.

Q. Did I do my utmost endeavour, as an officer, to bring them to action during those days?

A. To the best of my knowledge you did, with unremitting assiduity.

Q. Had you commanded a British fleet, and in the situation the French fleet were in with respect to the fleet; under my command, wind and weather as it then was, would you have hesitated one moment, to have gone down and attacked them?

A. To the best of my remembrance, and to the best of my judgment, if I had the honour of commanding a British fleet under such circumstances, I could not have desired a better opportunity than what daily offered, to have given battle to an enemy turning up towards me, and endeavouring, as the British fleet actually did, to bring an action.

Q. As I am charged with advancing towards the enemy On the 27th of July; and made the signal for battle, without forming the line; what in your judgment would have been the consequence if I had formed it, instead of closing with them as I did?

A. Judging of their future conduct by the past, had the Admiral formed his fleet in a line of battle, on the 27th in the morning, I do not think we could have brought them to action at all; and even without forming the line, had it not been for a shift of wind, I do not think we should have fetched near enough within cannon shot of any part of their fleet.

Q. How many ships had the Vice Admiral of the red with him advancing towards the enemy, on the larboard tack, after the action?

A. I really do not positively recollect.

Q. Was your ship one of them?

A. I was one of the number that followed Sir Robert Harland towards the rear of the fleet, in the Stirling Castle, which I had then the honour to command.

Q. I am charged with having hauled down the signal for battle, by which the red division was prevented from renewing the fight upon the larboard tack; I desire you would acquaint the Court, what in your judgment would have been the consequence, if by keeping abroad that signal, or making any other, I had ordered the Vice Admiral of the red to advance with the ships at that time to the attack?

A. To the best of my judgment, such a measure would have been very disadvantageous to the red division, for such a part only of the fleet, was not of sufficient force to nave attacked the whole of the French fleet, and moreover they were not close up together.

Q. Did you see the French fleet wear and begin to form their line on the starboard tack?

A. I do recollect to have seen a part of the French fleet, I cannot say the whole, making sail ahead on the larboard tack, and some of them formed themselves into a line of battle ahead, but I cannot say exactly at what time; there were more, but I cannot fix how many of them were formed at the time I allude to.

Q. I am charged with having wore to stand to the southward at this time, and leading the British fleet directly from the enemy; did my wearing at this time appear to you to be a necessary manoeuvre, or had I the appearance of a flight?

122

A. Your wearing to the southward appeared to me to see a most necessary measure, nor had it surely by any means the appearance of a flight, nor did it ever in the smallest degree make an impression upon me to that effect?

Q. *What sail was you under during the night of the 27th?*

A. During the night of the 27th, in general double reefed topsails and mizzen stay sail, sometimes the fore tack was abroad, the foresail very often hauled up, much to the fatigue of my ship's company; my ship was foul, and I could not use the common expedient of backing my mizzen topsail, for fear of driving down to leeward, and putting the fleet into confusion. I don't recollect how often the foresail was hauled down, but it was very often; my main top mast having been shot thro' above and below the cap, and the bowsprit two turns into the near gammon-, I did not dare to let a reef out to follow my Admiral, so fast as I otherwise mould have done. I thought it better to compromise with the weather to preserve my mast with double reefed topsails, than run the risque of having my mall carried away. I now allude retrospectively to my having followed Sir Robert Harland. Sometimes we hauled aft the main top mast stay fail sheet, and once or twice hoisted the fore top mast stay fail; now I hope I have been sufficiently minute.

Q. *From the very bad failing of your ship, did it not occasion your falling so far astern of the Red division, as to mix with the centre division?*

A. Not that I remember.

Q. *Did you, during the night of the 27th, and at what time of the night, call your men to quarters, upon a ship's ranging up nearly with you, which you thought was a ship of the enemy?*

A. At or about the first dawning of the day, having my leader the Berwick in my eye, coveting to keep myself to windward, and being then actually upon her weather quarter, that I might have it in my power to assume my exact place with more precision in the line of battle, as day light should advance, I observed a ship ranging up upon my weather quarter. When first I law her, I think about three points upon the weather quarter, not knowing who it might be, I thought it prudent to order my ship, company to their quarters, and resume our preparation for battle, which had been for some time discontinued.

Q. *What ship was it?*

A. As that ship approached towards our beam, I could plainly discern a flag at her fore top mast head, the lour thereof I could not yet ascertain with certainty j palling further along, and no act of hostility having passed betwixt us, I presumed it to be the Formidable, although she had neither top nor poop light, nor ensign flying, nor no light at her bowsprit end. About this time 1 bore up a little, as the day opened, and I could do it with safety, to get more precisely into my station in the line of battle. The ship in question still passing along, until he came further forward, and then I observed her having her ensign flying. Seeing a ship approach us in the morning as this did, I confess I was not without some apprehension that the enemy had, by stretching away on the larboard tack, doubled upon our rear in order to regain the windward gage; and at or about the fame time, feeing other ships in the fame quarter of the compass, my suspicions grew stronger in that respect, insomuch that I ruminated and entertained a thought of making the signal for seeing strange ships in the N. W. quarter. I had proceeded so far in my own mind, as to be pondering whether to make the day or night signal, which nearly fixes the time of my being under that apprehension.

Q. Did you see the lights of the Admiral of your own division at that time?

A. I do not recollect that circumstance.

Q. When day came, was you then lure it was the Vice Admiral of the Blue that you had seen before?

A. To the best of my knowledge and remembrance it could be no other.

Q. On the 28th if I had chased towards Ushant, in the condition the fleet were in after the action of the 28th, in their masts and yards, was there the least probability of coming up with the French fleet before they had reached the port of Brest?

A. Had the French fleet observed their former line of conduct, there could not be the least probability of your conning up with them before they reached the port of Brest. By their line of conduct I mean constantly avoiding an engagement.

Q. You have heard all the articles of the charge, therefore I desire you will state to the Court any instance, if you saw or know of any such, in which I negligently performed my duty, or any part of it, either on the 27th or 28th of July?

A. I did not observe any thing done or left undone by Admiral Keppel, on the 27th or 28th of July, bearing the appearance or his negligently performing his duty.

Sir Charles ordered to withdraw.

APPENDIX G
THE OPPOSING FLEETS
AT THE BATTLE OF THE SAINTS

THE BRITISH FLEET

Ships	Guns	Captains
	VAN	
Marlborough	74	Taylor Penny
Arrogant	74	Samuel Cornish
Alcide	74	Charles Thompson
Nonsuch	74	William Truscott
Conqueror	74	George Balfour
Princesse	70	Samuel Drake, Rear-Admiral Charles Knatchbull
Prince George	98	James Williams
Torbay	74	John Gidoin
Anson	64	William Blair
Janie	74	Robert Barber
Russel	74	James Saumarez
	CENTER	
America	64	Samuel Thompson
Hercules	74	Henry Savage
Prothee	64	Charles Buckner

Resolution	74	Robert Manners
Agamemnon	64	Benjamin Caldwell
Duke	98	Alan Gardner
Formidable	98	G.B. Rodney, Admiral **Sir Charles Douglas,** John Symonds, Lord Cranstoun
Namur	90	C. Inglis
St. Albans	64	William Cornwallis
Canada	74	Thomas Dumaresq
Repulse	64	N. Charrington
Ajax	74	Robert Fanshawe
Bedford	74	E. Affleck, Commodore Thomas Graves

REAR

Prince William	64	GeorgeWilkinson
Magnificent	74	Robert Linzee
Centaur	74	John Inglefield
Belliqueuse	64	Alexander Sutherland
Warrior	74	James Wallace
Monarch	74	Francis Reynolds
Barfleur	90	Samuel Hood, Vice-Admiral John Knight
Valiant	74	G.S. Goodall
Yarmouth	64	A. Parry
Montagu	74	George Bowen
Alfred	74	W. Bayne
Royal Oak	74	Thomas Burnett

THE FRENCH FLEET

Ships	Guns	Captains
BLUE (THIRD) SQUADRON		
Hercule	74	Chadeau de la Clocheterie
Souverain	74	de Glandevez
Palmier	74	de Martelly-Chautard
Northumberland	74	de Sainte-Cesaire
Neptune	74	Renaud d'Aleins
Auguste	80	de Bougainville, R-Admiral de Castellan
Ardent	64	de Gouzillon
Scipion	74	de Chavel
Brave	74	d'Amblimont
Citoyen	74	d'Ethy
WHITE (FIRST) SQUADRON		
Hector	74	de la Vicomte
Cesar	74	de Marigny
Dauphin-Royal	70	de Roquefeuil-Montperoux
Languedoc	80	d'Arros d'Argelos
Ville de Paris	104	Comte de Grasse, Admiral de Lavilleon de Vaugirauld
Couronne	80	Mithon de Genouilly
Eveille	64	le Gardeur de Tilly
Sceptre	74	de Vaudreuil
Glorieux	74	d'Escars
BLUE (SECOND) SQUADRON		
Diademe	74	de Monteclerc
Destin	74	Dumaitz de Goimpy
Magnanime	74	le Begue
Reflechi	64	de Medine

Conquerant	74	de la Grandiere
Magnifique	74	Macarthy Macteigne
Triomphant	80	de Vaudreuil, Vice Admiral du Pavillon
Bourgogne	74	de Charitte
Duc-de-Bourgogne	80	Coriolis d'Espinouse De Champmartin
Marseillais	74	de Castellane Majastre
Pluton	74	d'Albert de Rions

BIBLIOGRAPHY

Adams, Max. *Trafalgar's Lost Hero: Admiral Lord Collingwood and the Defeat of Napoleon.* Hoboken, NJ: Wiley, 2005.

Adams, W. H. Davenport. *Eminent Sailors: a Series of Biographies of Great Naval Commanders, Including an Historical Sketch of the British Navy from Drake to Collingwood.* London: George Routledge and Sons, 1882. Internet: accessed through Google Books at http://books.google.com

Alison, Archibald. *History of Europe from the Commencement of the French Revolution in 1789 to the Restoration of the Bourbons in 1815.* Ninth Edition, Vol. III. Edinburgh: William Blackwood and Sons, 1854. Internet: accessed through Google Books at http://books.google.com

Anderson, William. *The Scottish Nation: or, the Sunames, Families, Liturature, Honours, and Biographical History of the People of Scotland,* vol. 1. A. Fullarton & Co., 1862. Internet: accessed through Google Books at http://books.google.com

Baxter, James Phinney. *The British Invasion from the North: The Campaigns of Generals Carleton and Burgoyne from Canada, 1776-1777, with the Journal of Lieut. William Digby, of the 53rd, or Shropshire Regiment of Foot.* Albany, NY: Joel Munsell's Sons, 1887. Internet: Accessed online through Google Books at http://books.google.com.

Black, Jeremy. *Britain as a Military Power, 1688-1815.* London: University College London Press, 1999. Accessed through the APUS Online Research Library.

--------. *European Warfare, 1660-1815.* London: University College London Press, 1994. Accessed through the APUS Online Research Library.

Bratten, John R. *The Gondola Philadelphia and the Battle of Lake Champlain*. College Station: Texas A&M University Press, 2002.

Breen, Kenneth. "George Bridges, Lord Rodney." *Precursors of Nelson: British Admirals of the Eighteenth Century*. Richard Harding and Peter LeFevre (eds.). Mechanicsburg, PA: Stockpole Books, 2000.

Brougham, Henry Lord. *The Life and Times of Henry Lord Brougham*. New York: Harper & Brothers, Publishers, 1871. Internet: accessed through Google Books at http://books.google.com

Brown, Stephen R. *Scurvy: How a Surgeon, a Mariner, and Gentleman Solved the Greatest Medical Mystery of the Age of Sail*. New York: Thomas Dunne Books, 2003.

Burke's Peerage and Baronetage, 96th Edition. London: Burke's Peerage Ltd., 1938.

Carre, Walter Riddell. *Border Memories; or, Sketches of Prominent Men and Women of the Border*. Edinburgh: James Thin, South Bridge, 1876. Internet: accessed through Google Books at http://books.google.com

Chambers, Robert and Thomas Thomson. *A Biographical Dictionary of Eminent Scotsmen*. Glasgow: Blackie and Son, 1855.

Charnock, John. *Biographia Navalis; or Impartial Memoirs of the Lives and Characters of Officers of the Navy of Great Britain from the Year 1660 to the Present Time*, vol. VI. London: R. Faulder, 1798. Internet: accessed through Google Books at http://books.google.com

Chesney, Col. Francis Rawdon. *Observations on the Past and Present State of Fire-Arms, and on the Probable Effects in War of the New Musket*. London: Longman, Brown, Green, and Longmans, 1852. Internet: accessed through Google Books at http://books.google.com

Clark, William Bell (ed.). *Naval Documents of the American Revolution*, vol. III-V. Washington: U.S. Government Printing Office, 1968-1970.

"Clerk, John of Eldin." *Dictionary of National Biography*. Vol. XI. Leslie Stephens (ed.). New York: MacMillan and Co., 1887. Internet: accessed through Google Books at http://books.google.com

Clerk, John. *An Essay on Naval Tactics, Systematical and Historical, with Explanatory Plates*. Third Edition. Edinburgh:

Adam Black, 1827. Internet: accessed online through Google Books at: http://books.google.com/books?id=LsdPpUcY xD4C&pg=PR1&dq=%22john+clerk%22+%22essay+on+naval +tactics%22+eldin

Conway, Stephen. "'A Joy Unknown for Years Past': The American War, Britishness and the Celebration of Rodney's Victory at the Saints." *History*, April 2001, Vol. 86, Issue 282. London. Accessed online through Proquest at http://search.ebscohost. com.ezproxy.apus.edu/login.aspx?direct=true&db=aph&AN=4 511560&site=ehost-live.

Corbett, Julian S. *Signals and Instructions, 1776-1794.* London: Navy Records Society, 1908. Elibron Classics reprint, 2005.

Cumberland, Richard. *Memoirs of Richard Cumberland,* Vol. II. London: Lackington, Allen, and Co., 1807. Internet: accessed through Google Books at http://books.google.com.

Currie, James, M.D., *Memoir of the Life, Writings, and Corre-spondence of James Currie, M.D. F.R.S. of Liverpool*, vol. II, William Wallace Currie, ed.. London: Longman, Rees, Orme, Brown, and Green, 1831. Internet: accessed through Google Books at http://books.google.com.

Distinguished Men of Modern Times (in Four Volumes), Vol. III. London: Charles Knight & Co., 1888. No author credited. Internet: accessed through Google Books at http://books. google.com.

Douglas, Charles. "An Account of the Result of Some Attempts Made to Ascertain the Temperature of the Sea in Great Depths, Near the Coasts of Lapland and Norway; as Also Some Anec-dotes, Collected in the Former. By Charles Douglas Esquire, F.R.S. Then Captain of His Majesty's Ship the Emerald, Anno 1769. *Philosophical Transactions (1683-1775),* Vol. 60, pp. 39-45. London: The Royal Society. Internet: accessed through JSTOR at http://www.jstor.org/stable/105875.

Douglas, General Sir Howard. *A Treatise on Naval Gunnery.* Lon-don: John Murray, Albemarle Street, 1860. Elibron classics reprint, 2007.

--------. *Naval Evolutions: A Memoir Containing a Review and Refutation of the Principal Essays and Arguments Advocat-ing Mr. Clerk's Claims, in Relation to the Manoeuvre of the 12th of April 1782; and Vindicating, by Tactical Demonstra-tion, and Numerous Authentic Documents, the Professional Skill of the British Officers Chiefly Concerned on that Memo-rable Occasion.* London: Thomas and William Boone, 1832.

University of Michigan reprint under the Michigan Historical Reprint Series.

--------. "On Naval Tactics." *The Edinburgh New Philosophical Journal, Exhibiting a View of the Progressive Discoveries and Improvements in the Sciences and the Arts*, October 1832 – April 1833. Jameson, Robert (ed.). Edinburgh: Adam and Charles Black, 1833. Internet: accessed through Google Books at http://books.google.com

Douglas, W.A.B. "Sir Charles Douglas," *Dictionary of Canadian Biography Online.* Internet: http://www.biographi.ca/en/ShowBio.asp?BioId=35982&query

Duffy, Michael. "Samuel Hood, First Viscount Hood." *Precursors of Nelson: British Admirals of the Eighteenth Century*, Richard Harding and Peter LeFevre (eds.). Mechanicsburg, PA: Stockpole Books, 2000.

Ekin, Charles. *The Naval Battles of Great Britain*. London: Baldwin and Cradock, 1828. Internet: Accessed online at Google Books: http://books.google.com.

Fleming, Thomas. "Unlikely Victory: Thirteen Ways the Americans Could Have Lost the Revolution," *What if?The World's Foremost Military Historians Imagine What Might Have Been.* Cowley, Robert, editor. New York: Berkely Books, 1999.

Fowler, William M., Jr. *Rebels Under Sail: The American Navy during the Revolution.* New York: Charles Scribner's Sons, 1976.

Fullom, S.W. *Life of General Sir Howard Douglas, Bart.: From his Notes, Conversations, and Correspondence.* London: John Murray, Albemarle St., 1863.

Gat, Azar. *A History of Military Thought, from the Enlightenment to the Cold War.* New York: Oxford University Press, USA, 2001.

Gates, David. *Warfare in the Nineteenth Century.* Hampshire, England: Palgrove, 2001. Accessed through the APUS Online Research Library.

"General Urquhart." *Public Characters of 1803-1804.* London: Richard Philips, 1804 (Elibron Classics Edition, 2005).

The Georgian Era: Memoirs of the Most Eminent Persons, Who Have Flourished in Great Britain, from the Accession of George the First to the Demise of George the Fourth, in Four Volumes.Volume II. London: Vizetelly, Branston and Co.,

1833. Internet: accessed through Google Books at http://books.google.com

Grant, James. *Old and New Edinburgh: Its History its People, and its Places,* vol. VI. Edinburgh: Cassell & Company, Ltd. Internet: accessed through Google Books at http://books.google.com

"Great Ships: Ships of the Line." *The Royal Navy.* Monte Markham, producer and director. A&E Television Networks, 1996. Television program.

Griffith, Samuel B. *The War for American Independence: from 1760 to the Surrender at Yorktown in 1781.* Illinois: Jane Griffith and Belle Gordon Griffith Heneberger, 2002.

Gwyn, Julian. *Ashore and Afloat: The British Navy and the Halifax Naval Yard Before 1820.* Ottowa: University of Ottowa Press, 2004, pp. 84-85.

-------- *Frigates and Foremasts: the North American Squadron in Nova Scotia Waters, 1745-1815.* Vancouver: UBC Press, 2003. Accessed through the APUS Online Research Library.

Hadden, James M. *Hadden's Journal and Orderly Books: a Journal Kept in Canada and Upon Burgoyne's Campaign in 1776 and 1777.* Albany, NY: Joel Munsell's Sons, 1884. Internet: accessed through Google Books at http://books.google.com

Hagan, Kenneth J. *This People's Navy: The Making of American Sea Power.* New York: The Free Press, 1991.

Hamner, Robert D. *Epic of the Dispossessed: Derek Walcott's Olmeros.* Columbia, MO: University of Missouri Press, 1997.

Hannay, David. *English Men of Action: Rodney.* London: McMillan and Co., 1891. Internet: accessed through Google Books at http://books.google.com

-------- (ed.). *Letters Written by Sir Samuel Hood (Viscount Hood) in 1781-2-3, Vol. III.* London: Publications of the Naval Records Society, 1895. Elibron Classics reprint, 2007.

Harding, Richard and Peter LeFevre. *Precursors of Nelson: British Admirals of the Eighteenth Century.* Mechanicsburg, PA: Stockpole Books, 2000.

Harding, Richard. *Seapower and Naval Warfare from 1650-1830.* London: University College London Press, 1999. Accessed through the APUS Online Research Library.

Herman, Arthur. *To Rule the Waves: How the British Navy Shaped the Modern World*. New York: Harper Perennial, 2004.

Hille, Julius Friedrich von, and Helga Doblin (translator). *The American Revolution, Garrison Life in French Canada and New York: Journal of an Officer in the Prinz Fredrich Regiment, 1776-1783*. Westport, CT: Greenwood Press, 1993.

James, W.M. *The British Navy in Adversity: A Study of the War of American Independence*. London: Longmans, Green and Co., 1933.

Kennedy, Paul. *The Rise and Fall of British Naval Mastery*. London: Penguin Books, 1976.

Lambert, R.S. *Redcoat Sailor: The Adventures of Sir Howard Douglas*. Toronto: MacMillan, 1956.

Laughton, Sir John Knox (ed.). *Letters and Papers of Charles, Lord Barham, Admiral of the Red Squadron, 1758-1813*. London: Navy Records Society, 1907. Internet: accessed through Google Books at http://books.google.com

Le Moine, J. M. Quebec, *Past and Present: A History of Quebec, 1608-1876*. Quebec: Augustin Cote & Co., 1876. Internet: accessed through Google Books at http://books.google.com

Leckie, Robert. *George Washington's War: The Saga of the American Revolution*. New York: Harper Perenial/Harper Collins, 1992.

Leneman, Leah. "Defamation in Scotland, 1750-1800." *Continuity and Change*, Number 15 (2). United Kingdom: Cambridge University Press, 2000.

Lewis, Charles Lee. *Admiral de Grasse and American Independence*. Annapolis, MD: U.S. Naval Institute, 1945.

Library World: A Medium of Intercommunication for Librarians, Vol. VIII, July, 1905 to June, 1906. London: Library Supply Co., 1906. Internet: accessed through Google Books at http://books.google.com

"*Life and Correspondence of the Late Admiral Lord Rodney*, by Major-General Mundy." *The Eclectic Review*, February, 1831. London: Holdsworth and Ball, 1831. Book review. Internet: accessed through Google Books at http://books.google.com

Lockhart, John Gibson. *Memoirs of Sir Walter Scott*. London: MacMillan and Co., 1900. Internet: accessed through Google Books at http://books.google.com

Mahan, Alfred Thayer. *The Influence of Sea Power Upon History, 1660-1783*. New York: Barnes & Noble Books, 2004. Originally published in 1890.

--------. *Major Operations of the Navies in the War of Independence*. Gloucestershire, UK: Nonsuch Publishing Ltd, 2006. Originally published in 1913.

---------. *Types of Naval Officers Drawn from the History of the British Navy*. Boston: Little, Brown, and Company, 1901. Internet: accessed through Google Books at http://books.google.com

Martin, James Kirby. *Benedict Arnold, Revolutionary Hero: An American Warrior Reconsidered*. New York: New York University Press, 1997.

Miller, Nathan. *Broadsides: The Age of Fighting Sail, 1775-1815*. New York: John Wiley & Sons, 2001.

-------. *Sea of Glory: A Naval History of the American Revolution*. Charleston, SC: The Nautical & Aviation Publishing Company of America, 1974.

"Memoirs of Sir Charles Douglas." *The Gentleman's and London Magazine: or Monthly Chronologer*, 1791 (London). Internet: accessed through Google Books at http://books.google.com.

Morgan, William James (ed.). *Naval Documents of the American Revolution*, vol. VI. Washington: U.S. Government Printing Office, 1972.

Morley, Vincent. *Irish Opinion and the American Revolution, 1766-1783*. Cambridge: Cambridge University Press, 2002. Accessed through the APUS Online Research Library.

Munday, John. *Naval Cannon*. Aylesbury, UK: Shire Publications Ltd, 1987.

Mundy, Major-General Godfrey Basil. *The Life and Correspondence of the Late Admiral Lord Rodney, Vol. II*. London: John Murray, 1830. Elibron Classics reprint, 2007.

National Maritime Museum, Greenwich. Internet: accessed online at http://www.nmm.ac.uk/memorials/Memorial.cfm?Search=douglas&MemorialID=M560

The Naval Chronicle for 1805: Containing a General and Biographical History of the Royal Navy of the United Kingdom; with a Variety of Original Papers of Nautical Subjects. London: I. Gold, 1805. Internet: Accessed online through Google Books at http://books.google.com.

Nelson, James L. *Benedict Arnold's Navy*. Camden, Maine: International Marine/McGraw-Hill, 2006.

Osler, Edward. *The Life of Admiral Viscount Exmouth*. London: BiblioBazaar, 2007 (original copyright 1854).

Palmer, Michael A. *Command at Sea: Naval Command and Control since the Sixteenth Century*. Cambridge, MA: Harvard University Press, 2005.

Paton, Thomas S. *Reports of Cases Decided in the House of Lords upon Appeal from Scotland from 1753 to 1813, Volume III*. Edinburgh: T&T Clark, 1853. Accessed online through Google Books at: http://books.google.com/books?id=9HE2AAA AIAAJ &pg=PA460&dq=sir+charles+douglas+ scotland+cases&lr=

Pearson, Michael. *Those Damned Rebels: The American Revolution as Seen Through British Eyes*. Da Capo Press, 1972.

Playfair, John. "On the Naval Tactics of the Late John Clerk, Esq. of Eldin." *The Works of John Playfair*, Vol. III.. Edinburgh: Archibald Constable & Co., 1822.

Potter, E.B. (ed.). *Sea Power*. Annapolis: Naval Institute Press, 1981.

Ramsden, Lady Guendolen. *Correspondence of Two Brothers: Edward Adolphus, Eleventh Duke of Somerset, and His Brother, Lord Webb Seymour, 1800 to 1819 and After*. London: Longmans, Green and Co, 1906. Internet: Accessed online through Google Books at http://books.google.com.

Reynolds, Clark G. *Navies in History*. Annapolis: Naval Institute Press, 1998.

Robertson, David. *A Treatise on the Rules of the Law of Personal Succession, in the Different Parts of the Realm; and on the Cases Regarding Foreign and International Succession, Which Have Been Decided in the British Courts.*

Robison, Rear Admiral S.S. *History of Naval Tactics from 1530 to 1930: The Evolution of Tactical Maxims*. Annapolis, MD: The United States Naval Institute, 1942.

Rodger, N.A.M. "Commissioned Officers' Careers in the Royal Navy, 1690-1815," *Journal for Maritime Research* (June 2001). Internet: http://www.jmr.nmm.ac.uk/server? show-=ConJmr Article.52&setPaginate=No

Rodger, N.A.M. *The Wooden World: An Anatomy of the Georgian Navy*. New York: W.W. Norton & Company, 1986.

"Rodney's Battle of 12th April, 1782: A Statement of Some Important Facts, Supported by Authentic Documents, Relating to the Operation of Breaking the Enemy's Line, as Practiced for the First Time in the Celebrated Battle of 12th April, 1782." *Quarterly Review*, vol. XLII, no. LXXXIII, January & March, 1830. London: John Murray, Albemarle Street, 1830. No author credited. Internet: accessed through Google Books at http://books.google.com

The Scots Magazine and Edinburgh Literary Miscellany, Vol. LXXI. Edinburgh: Archibald Constable and Company, 1809.

Scott, Sir Walter. *Life of Napoleon Bonaparte*, Vol 3. Edinburgh: A. & C. Black, 1873. Internet: accessed through Google Books at http://books.google.com

"Sea Power." *Proceedings of the United States Naval Institute*. Annapolis, MD: U.S. Naval Institute, 1893. Reprinted from *London Times and Fortnightly Review*.

"Sir Charles Douglas's Strathspey." All Songs Considered at *NPR.org*. Internet: accessed online at http://www.npr.org/templates/story/story.php?storyId=18882029.

Stairs, W. J. and Susan Morrow Stairs. *Family History: Stairs, Morrow, Including Letters, Diaries, Essays, Poems, etc.* Halifax, Nova Scotia: McAlpine Publishing Company, Ltd., 1906.

Stephens, Alexander. *Public Characters of 1800-1801*. London: Printed for Richard Phillips by T. Gillet, 1801.

Trew, Peter. *Rodney and the Breaking of the Line*. South Yorkshire, England: Pen and Sword, 2006.

The Trial of the Honorable Augustus Keppel, Admiral of the Blue Squadron, at a Court Martial. Recorded by Thomas Blandemor. Portsmouth: Wilkes, Breadhower, and Peadle, 1779.

Tunstall, Brian. *Naval Warfare in the Age of Sail: The Evolution of Fighting Tactics, 1650-1815*. Edited by Dr. Nicholas Tracy. Edison, NJ: Wellfleet Press, 2001. Originally published in Great Britain in 1990 by Conway Maritime Press.

United Service Journal and Naval Military Magazine, 1830 Part 1. London: Henry Colburn and Richard Bentley, 1830. Compilation. Internet: accessed through Google Books at http://books.google.com

Wallace, A.J.B. "A British Officer in Active Service, 1799." *The Annual of the British School at Athens*, Vol. 23. British School at Athens, 1918/1919. Internet: accessed through JSTOR at http://www.jstor.org/stable/30096857.

Watkins, John. *The Life and Times of "England's Patriot King," William the Fourth: With a Brief Memoir of Her Majesty Queen Adelaide, and Her Family.* London: Fisher, Son & Jackson, 1831. Internet: accessed through Google Books at http://books.google.com

White, Thomas. *Naval Researches; or a Candid Inquiry into the Conduct of Admirals Byron, Graves, Hood and Rodney, in the Actions off Grenada, Chesapeak, St. Christophers, and of the Ninth and Twelfth of April, 1782.* Boston: Gregg Press, 1972. Reprint, originally published in London by Whittaker, Treacher, and Arnott in 1830.

Wilson, Barry K. *Benedict Arnold: a Traitor in Our Midst.* Montreal: McGill-Queen's University Press, 2001. Accessed through the APUS Online Research Library.

"Wooden Walls." *The Royal Navy.* Jason Markham and Monte Markham, producers. A&E Television Networks, 2002. Television program.

Würtele, Fred C. (ed.). *Blockade of Quebec in 1775-1776 by the American Revolutionsists.* Port Washington, NY: Kennikat Press, 1970.

ABOUT THE AUTHOR

CHRISTOPHER VALIN

Christopher J. Valin is a writer, artist, historian, and teacher living in the Los Angeles area with his wife and two children. He received his Master's Degree with Honors in Military History with a concentration in American Revolution Studies from American Military University, his Bachelor's Degree in History from the University of Colorado at Colorado Springs, and his teaching degree from Regis University. Christopher has been writing in many forms since he was a child, including short stories, screenplays, and comic books, for which he has also worked as an artist. His short stories have appeared in two anthologies: *The Artifact: An Anthology* and *Keys: Unlocking the Universe*. His reviews of television shows and movies have appeared on various websites, including PopSyndicate.com, Mediasharx.com, and ZENtertainment.com.

Christopher was the winner of Part 9 of the Cowrite Screenwriting Contest, Chapter 16 of the *L.A. Times* "Birds of Paradise" Collaborative Novel Contest, and Week 3 of the FanLib.com *Kirk vs. Picard* Screenwriting Contest, and his other screenplays and teleplays have won or placed in several other competitions, including the Scriptwriters' Network Producers Outreach Program, the Nicholl Fellowship in Screenwriting, the Chesterfield Fellowship Screenwriting Competition, the Fade In Awards, the Screenwriting Expo Cyberspace Open, the Austin Film Festival Screenwriting Contest, Scriptapalooza, and Scriptapalooza TV.

Christopher Valin is also the 5x great-grandson of the subject of this book— Sir Charles Douglas.

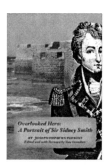

OVERLOOKED HERO:
A Portrait of Sir Sidney Smith
by Joseph Hepburn Parsons
**Edited and with Forward by
Tom Grundner**

Lost for almost 100 years
An engaging portrait of the man who is arguably the greatest Admiral of the Napoleonic Wars
Sir Sidney Smith

Everyone knows the two greatest heroes and the two greatest battles of the Napoleonic Wars. They were Admiral Horatio Nelson's victory at Trafalgar, and Field Marshall Arthur Wellesley's victory at Waterloo. However, it's entirely possible that there would have never been a Trafalgar or a Waterloo if it had not been for one man—Sir Sidney Smith.

Sir Sidney who?

Yes, exactly. That's the point of this book.

Joseph Parson paints an unforgettable portrait of a truly overlooked hero. It is not a history or a biography, as it makes no pretense at being exhaustive. Rather, in a short, easy to read, volume, he paints a vivid portrait of this man, and why he was so important.

"There is no way you can understand the Napoleonic Wars without understanding the contributions of Sir Sidney Smith—and this book is a great place to start."

DON'T MISS ALL OF THE EXCITING
BOOKS IN THE SIR SIDNEY SMITH SERIES
BY
TOM GRUNDNER

THE MIDSHIPMAN PRINCE

How do you keep a prince alive when the combined forces of three nations (and a smattering of privateers) want him dead? Worse, how do you do it when his life is in the hands of a 17 year old lieutenant, an alcoholic college professor, and a woman who has fired more naval guns than either of them? The first book in the Sir Sidney Smith nautical adventure series.

HMS DIAMOND

After surviving the horrors of the destruction of Toulon, Sir Sidney is given a critical assignment. British gold shipments are going missing. Even worse, the ships are literally disappearing in plain sight of their escorts and the vessels around them. The mystery must be solved, but to do that Sir Sidney must unravel a web of intrigue that leads all the way to the Board of Admiralty.

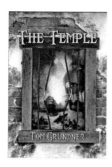

THE TEMPLE

Napoleon is massing ships, troops, and supplies at Toulon and a number of other ports. He is clearly planning an invasion; but an invasion of who, where, and when, no one knows. The key is a captured message, but it's encoded in a way that has never been seen before. From a dreary prison in Paris, to an opulent palace in Constantinople, to the horror of the Battle of the Nile—The Temple will take you on a wild ride through 18th Century history.

AND DON'T MISS THE FOURTH BOOK
IN THIS THRILLING SERIES COMING IN 2010

ACRE

From Fireship Press
www.FireshipPress.com

All Fireship Press books are available directly through our website, amazon.com, via leading bookstores from coast-to-coast, and from all major distributors in the U.S., Canada, the UK, and Europe.

LaVergne, TN USA
30 November 2009
165526LV00005B/95/P